Whickwithy

Sentience

All rights reserved

Copyright © 2017 Whickwithy

This book may not be reproduced in whole or in part in any form.

Published by Whickwithy

PO Box 2375, Scarborough, ME 04070

whickwithy@gmail.com

ISBN: 978-0-997-1412-0-7

Sentience by Whickwithy

Available for bookstores in most countries

Printed and bound by Ingram-Sparks

Available online at Amazon

Printed and bound by Createspace

First published in 2017

Whickwithy

SENTIENCE

changes everything...

by Whickwithy

This book is dedicated to two very special women without whom this book never would have been written. No, it is not Simone de Beauvoir or Eleanor Roosevelt. Or Ginger Rogers, for that matter.

"Power at its most vicious is a riposte to powerlessness."
- Simone de Beauvoir

"Great minds discuss ideas; average minds discuss events; small minds discuss people."
- Eleanor Roosevelt

"Sure he (Fred Astaire) was great, but don't forget that Ginger Rogers did everything he did, ...backwards and in high heels."
- Bob Thaves, "Frank and Ernest" comic strip

"Darkness cannot drive out darkness; only light can do that.
Hate cannot drive out hate; only love can do that."
- Martin Luther King, Jr.

"And nothing natural is evil"
-Marcus Aurelius

We have so far missed a key ingredient for becoming genuinely, firmly sentient. Sapience is still a distant dream.

The human race's incessant emotional turmoil and unreason is not inherent. Both are legacies of a single mistake on our way to sentience.

I'd much rather be writing poetry.

Contents

Whickwithy

Foreword

It would help greatly when reading this book, to suspend the belief that all of the craziness of mankind is the natural order of things. That pattern of thought has been holding us back for millennia. All of the absurd aspects of human life are not required. The fundamental premise of this book is that it is absolutely *not* necessary that mankind's existence be plagued with all of the nonsensical behaviours that make human life something that is often just endured.

A rather common belief, reinforced by conditioning handed down to us, is that we are aberrant by design. That is a disastrous misbelief. The disruptive elements of human existence are not a necessity. We can live a life that is worth living as a race and as individuals: with reason. Unreason is a legacy, not a necessity.

There is a single misconception embedded in our subconscious that undermines everything we attempt. It needs to be recognized, acknowledged, and removed. Once it is, we will have removed a major obstacle to achieving maturity as a race.

The question that needs to be asked is why is it that humanity is so irrational, brutal, and violent? That is the first, most important question. The answer will surprise you.

Whickwithy

Whickwithy

In search of the nail

"For want of a nail the shoe was lost.
For want of a shoe the horse was lost.
For want of a horse the rider was lost.
For want of a rider the message was lost.
For want of a message the battle was lost.
For want of a battle the kingdom was lost.
And all for the want of a horseshoe nail."

The proverb above dates back many centuries portraying a situation in which the failure to correct a seemingly small, overall insignificant dysfunction leads, by successively critical stages, to an egregious outcome.

Just such a situation has plagued humanity since our earliest existence. We have focused on the battles, messages, and riders and paid little attention to the nail that causes a great deal of the disturbance to our nature. The missing nail that compromised our emergence into sentience disappeared in the distant mists of our first attempts at sentience.

We have focused on the results of our unreason, the messages, riders and battles, not the cause of our disruption. Until we find the nail that was lost we will never be whole. That time is now.

There must be something very peculiar about this nail. The inspection of its existence and acknowledgement of its absence have been continually and successfully impeded. It is like the river Lethe of Greek mythology that caused forgetfulness. The mind continually veers away from its consideration. The nail finally reached the point that it was no longer even considered. It was completely swept under the rug, never to be mentioned. The day-to-day disruptions to the kingdom finally became so prevalent as to distract us and prevent us from ever suspecting that mankind could have peace of mind and a satisfying, civilized existence.

We do not need to be the unreasonable, combative race that we have been so far. It is not a given. It is not our required destiny. It is only a legacy and the results of a mistake that was made long ago. As a race striving to be sentient, we need to remove this distortion to our existence and unfetter our awareness. Without the nail, the kingdom is lost.

The missing nail is something that was lacking long before mankind arrived on the scene. It only became apparent and important with the advent of sentience. We recognized the lack but could not find, and never truly accepted, the possibility of rectification. It has drifted along through our existence distorting all in its path. Clarity is within our reach. We need only recognize the existence of the missing nail, retrieve it and hammer it home.

We inadvertently hid the nail from scrutiny. We buried it under millennia of conditioning not realizing its importance. Unreason became an accepted burden with which mankind just lives. What was never understood was that the nail carries the weight of the world with it for a sentient race. The conditioning has had its own compromising effects and just continues to add weight to the burden.

Because of the missing nail, we have continued to perform, in many ways, as the animals that preceded us, thus stranding us somewhere between the animal state and the human state which holds more potential than we have ever imagined.

We obscured something that disturbed us in the desperate hope that it would all just go away. It will not go away until we find that nail. Our sentient awareness is relentless. Sentience is not a curse, misinformation is. We are faced with this misinformation almost every day of our adult lives and it unsettles us.

Our primitive ancestors despaired at the burden of sentience that made us aware of a lack that seems impossible to address. Sentience itself is often laid to blame. Unencumbered sentience is a gift beyond measure. We are no longer primitive, the lack is addressable. We will unfetter our sentience as well as our reason by recognizing this incongruity and addressing it.

We have spent most of mankind's efforts, over the millennia, combatting the results of unreason rather than the source. We chase after the nonsense that occurs at the surface, due to unreason, rather than unreason itself and its root cause. We have been completely ignoring the fact that unreason exists with no acceptable justification.

The misperceptions are nothing more than our ancient ancestor's excessive imagination, creativity, and story-telling ability brought to bear on what was, in the past, a seemingly insurmountable problem. It is no longer insurmountable.

Root cause means the ultimate source of a problem. In this particular case, there are layers and layers of secondary and tertiary problems that have developed over the millennia due to the initial root cause of unreason. This hides the root cause beneath a bewildering array of problems that seem of immediate importance but are far removed from the source of the problem.

These are what we attack. We attack the results of the disturbance, not the source of our unreason. At the core, at the very root, a great deal of the disturbance to our existence is due to a single lack that has stranded us somewhere between an animal's existence and what should be humanity's unchallenged sentient existence.

This book describes the nature and source of our unreason, our blindspot, as well as the solution. The obviousness of the problem, as well as the simplicity of the solution, are startling in retrospect. It would even be amusing except for the millennia that have past in which we have caused ourselves severe difficulties and suffering. The millennia that have past suggest just how deep the conditioning goes. It is not easy to overcome that conditioning and accept the premise. This need to be approached with great consideration.

Sentience

Sentience changed everything when it first emerged ... and we weren't prepared for it. Our distant ancestors made many mistakes in their initial attempts to wield sentience. The universe does not revolve around the earth, solar eclipses are not caused by angry gods. There was one mistake that they made, though, from which we have yet to recover and it was a big one. It has tumbled through our existence affecting everything in its path. We have veered far into the arms of unreason because of it.

We need just the slightest redirect to get sentience back on course, even after all of the millennia that have past. The change in course is breathtakingly simple and the end-effect tremendous. Our sentience will change everything, again.

While sentience has existed for as long as mankind, it really came into its own around three thousand years ago. At that time, mankind finally began to attempt to add reasoning and coherent thought to the hyperawareness of our sentient nature.

It was noted by multiple philosophers, during those first centuries in which we attempted reasoning, that something was wrong. Marcus Aurelius of the Roman Empire may have described it best as, while all of nature seemed at peace with itself, there was something suspicious concerning mankind's situation. Something was broken. The conclusion supported throughout the ages is that it is mankind itself that is broken. That is not so.

Unfortunately, the human race had already trained itself to ignore a particularly serious issue by the time reason had emerged. The boundaries of our problems had already blurred, while the most important problem faded into the background. We had blunted all of our suspicions to the elephant in the room. We convinced ourselves that the disruption was just a side-effect of becoming sentient. *Big mistake!* Sentience only fails when it has something to hide.

This issue we faced was not new. It had existed within the animal kingdom long before mankind. Humanity just had the wit, due to sentience, to recognize the issue. It has driven us to distraction ever since. The animals that preceded us did not have the wit to realize nor the sensitivity to care about this inconsistency in their existence. It did not disrupt a non-sentient species. It only became a serious problem in the presence of sentience. Sentience made it impossible to tolerate, so, it was buried and hidden from view.

By doing so, humanity disastrously reflected its animalistic origins rather than its humanistic potential. Animals may be able to hide from something that disturbs them, but mankind's sentient nature assures that we never can. It just wears away at our sanity instead.

The genesis of the mistake that mankind made was not realizing that something of import had changed when sentience was achieved. This caused our sentience to be blind-sided. We were unprepared to deal with the problem at the time. Now, finally, the problem will become obvious.

That is the thing about sentience. It is a potential, not a finished product. We took the worst possible approach to the problem. We reacted like a non-sentient race. We buried the problem. Our sentience grated against this inheritance without an easily recognized solution to its humbling effect, so it was allowed to slip past us. We let it get behind us.

Haven't you ever wondered why human existence is still such a struggle, such a mess, so haphazard, so aimless, so destructive? That is the first clue. We live in a rather benign universe. While the universe can certainly disrupt things with a vengeance, on the whole, it is rather complacent towards a developed sentient species. If we pay attention and use our innate intelligence, we can probably handle anything the universe throws at us, as long as we have time to prepare.

The universe does not cause our disruption. *The disruptions that we continue to incur are almost exclusively self-inflicted.* Mankind's worst enemy is itself. Another clue. Something unsettles us. Unreason distracts our attention. We are enfeebled. We lash out like a brute.

The universe lays open to a *sane*, sentient species, a species that does not seem intent on disrupting its own existence. If it wasn't for this single blindspot, mankind could be living a very acceptable existence rather than inflicting untold needless harm on itself.

Our view of life comes down to each individual's perception of existence. When one of those perceptions becomes common among many individuals in a society, it affects that society. The more people that accept a perception, the more it becomes the reality. In this case, due to the distant origins in time, the missing nail affects all of humanity. We deluded ourselves and we are still paying the price.

This particular disturbance infects all of what we do because it lies so very close to home. Something is missing and that loss has tumbled through our existence for more than three thousand years affecting everything it touches. It is the pebble that started the avalanche of unreason.

Success without all of the benefits

Even though we have succeeded beyond measure in this universe, we continue to be a race that is too mired in the depths of its own unreason and deceit. The rampant deceit is due to the perceived necessity to hide the nail. Because of our hampered sentience, the success is unbalanced. We continue to cause ourselves untold and unnecessary problems. We delude and deceive ourselves, sometimes blatantly because of the missing nail. The human race often acts like an unruly child. The danger and damage that this unruly child can cause is becoming more pronounced as our abilities progress.

The root cause of our problems is a very uncomfortable realization to inspect closely. It is easier to look at all of our superficial problems and attack them like a brute with little or no rational thought. That is not intelligence coming to the fore. That is despair having its way. It is human intelligence and sentience at war with itself. Human intelligence continues to be ruled by unreasoning fear like a common animal hounded by its own failure.

Another good analogy for the source of the problem is a keylog. When lumberjacks cut and transport logs by floating them down a river the logs can get jammed up rather than continue to float down the river. The solution to clearing the logjam is to identify the single, key log that can be removed to let the rest of the logs flow freely. The logjam caused by the missing nail is disrupting our sentience and restricting our clear view of a rather benign universe and full success within it. Removing the key log will free mankind's potential by releasing our intelligence and emotional stability. Mankind can finally be truly magnificent.

A lot of people point to war and say it should not exist. Very true but it is so close to the line "For want of a battle the kingdom was lost" as to be laughable. We dupe ourselves into believing that war and violence are the *big* problems because they are so blatant.

War and fretting about war are just a couple of the many ways we use to distract ourselves. War is clearly not *causing* our problems. It is a symptom, it is an outbreak of unreason on a tremendous scale. It is nowhere near the source of unreason. Declaring that war is a bad and that peace is good has no effect on anything as long as the irrationality of the human race continues.

War is so far down the chain of events and aberrations of mankind that it cannot rationally be considered the fundamental problem. Attempting to solve war or decree peace without looking deeper into what it is that disturbs the human race and its existence is futility in the extreme.

All of war and terrorism, all violence for that matter, is built on the feelings of instability and distrust of others that increases exponentially with social distance. It is reinforced with a ping pong-like build up of offenses from both parties, one after another, supported by underlying feelings of aggression and distrust. Like a fractal, this describes violence on any scale.

What causes all of these aggressive, verifiably insane feelings? Each step building to more anger and violence. The question is not who started it. The question is not who's right. The only real question is what puts us in such a state that we cannot see these points clearly and overcome them? Why do we lash out in anger and violence? What do we hide behind the facade of violence? From what are we attempting to distract ourselves? From where do the feelings of aggression come? The smokescreen of these behaviours are tantamount to a child's tantrum. What causes the tantrum? It is childish at best. It is a clue.

Why is it that we feel so insecure, so distracted, so hopeless of our state, that we react with violence? We have to get at the *root cause* of our instability, violence, and non-sentient, non-sapient behaviour. Pointing out that we are unstable, violent, and acting in a non-sentient manner does nothing without the deeper study. Anything less is just an admission and acceptance of the status quo. The overriding assumption is that we are so inherently disturbed that we just have violent tendencies and cannot rid ourselves of them. Therefore, we must just stop doing them. Can you see the child pouting?

There is a source for all of this disturbance. We will not remove the instability of mankind until we remove its primary source. Anything else is just another distraction. That is not good enough. Without the identification and removal of the source, we are just accepting the futility of our efforts, bowing down to the seemingly inevitable. Despair at our situation is the result. This has happened repeatedly throughout history. Each time we come closer to complete despair. 'Mankind is a brute, so live with it'. The finer qualities of the human character seem to get further and further from our grasp. The magnificence of mankind stalls. It seems easier to just stay brutish. It is not. It is a false flag.

Another of the misperceived surface culprits that is blamed for our problems dates back to our distant past. "Money is the root of all evil" is a deep abiding belief among many. Money is surely an important invention of mankind that allowed humanity to build a society beyond the hunter/gatherer and agrarian stage of existence. It is not money, in and of itself, that is the issue. It is the *perceptions* that sometimes develop concerning money that should come into question. What causes the aberration in the human character to obsess about money?

Another surface issue is the suggestion that mankind is just lazy or, more exactly, some people are just lazy. The facts don't really support this. Up until our fifties, the energy with which we *should* be able to pursue life is abundant. In children, it is very obvious that the energy is in overabundance. In many, something emerges to suppress that energy. Something develops to tap it and drains that energy. Something puts paid on any interest in life. There are plenty of inducements to passivity, such as cigarettes, food, alcohol, television, and other mindless pursuits. But, what induces us to become so distracted as to abandon the pursuit and celebration of life?

A flaw develops in many individuals as they physically mature into life. Unreason takes an unrelenting hold supplanting the celebration and honoring of life that should develop. Life, reason, and sentience are dismantled by this flaw in our perceptions. We learn to regards life as something less than our instincts tell us it should be. This distractions towards lethargy or some obsession are two primary extremes that replace the celebration of life. For most, the drudgery of life supplants the celebration of life. The drudgery of life is the norm today. It does not need to be.

Why would individuals seek items of limited value, such as money or power, in such an obsessive manner or just give up on life? What is missing in life to cause these obsessive behaviours that focus on one small part of existence? That the celebration and joy of life are replaced with an incessant need for justification of existence or despair is a signpost leading the way. Another clue.

Our obsessive pursuit of progress is another aberrant quality. While progress is, of course, important and necessary, our unreasoning pursuit of it is not. We do not always pursue progress as a means of improving the human race or our lives but more as an attempt to distract ourselves from something that we do not even recognize. The frantic nature of our pursuit of progress is suspicious indeed. It is like we are continually looking for something to make life worth living. Important clue.

It is not a sapient pursuit of progress. Many of the so-called improvements to our lives have little to do with improving the most important conditions of life, but enable the furtherance of efforts to distract from life. It is unbalanced.

It is as if we are attempting to outrun something that indistinctly stalks us. As if we are attempting to distance ourselves from some haunting shadow, lurking in obscurity, that continues to pursue us from behind. That something seems to whisper that we are not worthy of our sentience. We seem to be seeking justification for our existence.

Since we have been unable to acknowledge the disturbance of unreason, much less the source, we settle for improvements in our material conditions. The improvement of most significance that we require is our emotional composure, stability of our essential being.

Something concerning the root cause makes us extremely uncomfortable. Our inability to face this source of problems makes it clear that we want to force a solution without ever recognizing the root cause of the problems. We are so blinded that we would rather put up with the ongoing violence and disruption than face this scourge. We don't even want to acknowledge its existence. We just accept it as our burden to bear. We don't want to talk about it. What lack could be so distressing that we would tolerate untold disruption rather than expose the lack? Big clue.

Our ancient ancestors may have attempted to resolve the issue, but due to their minimal knowledge and insight, failed. It is also possible, though, that the disturbance was never consciously recognized but undermined their sentience in complete obscurity like a thief in the night. In either case, the eventual solution they attempted was to bury the problem. Now, we continually shy away from any mention of the disturbance because we have been conditioned to do so and we are uncertain of a remedy.

We continuously tinker with the systems of mankind. The institutions, and structures of humanity are also not the source of our problems. Again, it is an attempt to blind ourselves to where the problem really resides. The systems have a flaw because their builders have a wound. Endlessly tinkering with the systems will not resolve our problems. The disturbance in the systems is due to the behavioural disruption of the individuals populating the systems.

It is humanity itself that has a deep wound that must be healed. It is not the systems that succumb to brutishness, nihilism, narcissism, deceit, greed, avarice, corruption, combativeness, violence, misogyny, misanthropy, and sociopathy.

What is truly shocking, in retrospect, is that humanity perceives these less than admirable qualities as part of our nature. They are not. They are all symptoms of a serious problem at the heart of humanity that can be remedied. There is a burr under the saddle. It is not inherent in humanity as seems to be the most common belief.

In times of unrest, our animal nature comes to the fore. This is because we have retained the brute characteristics of our animal ancestry. This is only true because of the disruption to our existence. It is not our natural state.

While we gained the ability to sense far more than any previous animal, we have not been able to recognize the enormity of the conflict that we face accurately and, thus, shrug it off as just the way it is. Subconsciously, we have determined that it is something that must never see the light of day.

This confusion and disruption has gone on so long because of the way humanity clings to the teachings of the past. It has not been the most sentient or sapient approach to life. Again, the shadow of the scourge is seen. We are always adding and seldom scrutinizing, modifying, or removing any of the dictates passed on from our ignorant and excessively imaginative ancestors.

Deep inside, once we reach maturity, we know where the problem lies. We just don't want to face it. We are so inured to the idea that we never even recognize the significance of the upheaval it causes in our lives. It just seems like a burden we must bear without any realization of its mass effect on the mind and proclivities of mankind. Another clue. The two, the scourge and all of the problems of mankind have become perceived as detached from each other. They are not.

As young children, we are conditioned into a lot of beliefs about life before our critical faculties develop. These often nonsensical dictates are etched into the metal of our subconscious and passed on from generation to generation without question.

The latest generation's view of existence will always have some improvements over any generation preceding it. Each generation adds some new insights to the overall picture. Each generation is also slightly less befuddled by the nonsense from the past. But, it is an agonizingly slow process encumbered by the nonsense laid at the foundations of an individual's mindset before critical thinking develops. Also, under the auspices of the disturbance, more confusion is added with each generation. One step forward, two steps back.

The fundamental foundation of nonsense laid by the source of our unreason is that we had better never look closely at our own existence because we won't like what we see. That is futile. That is disastrous. That is just so wrong. Until our sentience overcomes this single disturbance, the nonsense will continue unimpeded.

Sentience matters

Sentience changes everything. It is a huge change for the animal life-form. That hyper-awareness clearly distinguishes humanity from the rest of the animal kingdom.

It is a unique adaptation. Unlike physical changes, sentience is something that is not suddenly complete and whole. It is not like the adaptation of the thumb. We did not immediately come into full possession of the use of our sentience and intellect. It began as a potential. It needed to be honed through accumulated knowledge, practice, and experience. It is a learning process.

We learn and we adapt. No other animal does that. It is a potential that we can use wisely or misuse disastrously. Amid our first steps into sentience, logic was useless without the essential data that was missing to arrive at rational conclusions.

The worst possible event for an emerging sentience would be to encounter something of tremendous import that could not be addressed in any way. That the universe rotated around the Earth was better than no answer at all. The only alternative when no answer sufficed would be to revert to the brutish mentality and attempt to bury the problem, hide it from those hyper-aware senses. Don't talk about it. That is exactly what happened and we have suffered for millennia.

The capabilities of sentience allow us to perceive - or misperceive existence in far more detail than any other form of life on earth. We ponder the galaxies and molecules, all aspects of existence.

Yet, we have a difficult time pondering the actions of the human race. Our own actions befuddle us, so we just accept it as being human. Another clue. Somehow, our own actions are bewildering and we have never been able to scrutinize the disturbing aspects of our actions or explain them. We just accept the unacceptable, unexplainable as part of our nature. Big, big mistake.

Our sentience has been inhibited since the very beginning because we have forced ourselves to misperceive a significant element of our existence and that disturbed the very foundations of our sentience.

It is no surprise that our most distant ancestors were confounded by their place in the world. They were attempting to understand and explain all of existence with little or no background knowledge. It would be more than surprising if they had interpreted everything correctly.

Throughout this book a number of humanity's views will be mentioned that are, in retrospect, topsy-turvy. Such as, women being sold short. That women have to battle for their rights at all is maybe the most significant clue as to the disturbance. How could that possibly make sense to a sentient race, or any race for that matter? There is something fundamentally wrong about the idea that women are not accepted as equals. You will see that clearly as we progress. So, why did we do it?

The actual disturbance to our existence occurred *because* we became a sentient race. We are not our ancestors, cringing in the dark from a problem that seemed too formidable. Their handling of the problem caused the conditioning that tells us to look away, it's bad; be afraid. We not only need to address the problem but, also, the many disturbing ramifications caused by its ongoing existence for millennia.

There is something grand about perceiving this universe with the greater clarity provided by sentience. It is the natural course of evolution. It is only the distortion to our clarity of sentience that makes us suffer.

In some ways, overcoming the distortion to our existence could be considered a right of passage, a necessary step to claim our sentience. More importantly, a gem of existence becomes more apparent than ever before as we approach this state of clarity. Altogether, once the whole situation is clearly understood, this gem stands to gain us an unrivaled satisfaction with existence.

We observe everything around us, in context to ourselves, to a higher degree than any animal has ever done before. The dichotomy between our animal origins and our brand-new (in cosmic terms) sentient state sent us off into the brambles. The disturbing knowledge seemed like a curse to our ancient ancestors; an insurmountable bane that we have never been able to face, much less resolve, until now. It seemed like an evil that had been unleashed on mankind for daring to think. Knowledge is not a curse, in and of itself, but the misinformation that was built around a certain piece of knowledge is a disaster of the highest order causing emotional instability, delusion, and disruption for the entire human race.

Homo sapiens

Our official name for the species, at this point, seems like nothing more than a bad joke. "Sapiens" indicates wisdom, or sapience. We certainly are not wise or even rational as a race. We are really hardly even sentient. Our sentience and intellect have been compromised. We cannot seem to get past the adolescent stage of existence.

Without a balanced emotional state, the race will continue to act like an out of control child. We create wonders and, yet, treat so much of our existence and our fellow man as unimportant. We create with one hand and destroy with the other. That is not sapient at all. That is not humanity's natural state.

If you look around at what we have wrought, there is something lacking. While we build amazing machines and systems, we have also caused a great deal of damage due to our emotional instability. It is not that there is something inherently wrong about emotions, it is that our emotional makeup is compromised.

One of the callsigns of the source of our unreason, that mistake made long ago, is that humanity has never been able to successfully regard itself. We don't even make the attempt. We accept the irrational components of our behaviour as inherent rather than look too closely at what is really going on. 'We are only human' may be the most disparaging, offensive, misleading comment since the beginning of our existence. There is something in the nature of mankind, when we look too closely, that we are extremely uncomfortable confronting. It is so disturbing that it is easier just to portray ourselves as a stumbling, bumbling race that "is only human". A clue.

What you will discover in this book is that mankind has a potential for magnificence that is much greater than our current circumstances portray. A single error has deluded us and diminished our existence to the point that the phase 'we are only human' is accepted without a second thought and just piled on top of plenty of other nonsense to explain our disturbed existence.

Many of our systems are in place to minimize the commotion caused by our perturbed behaviour. Legislation, legal systems, enforcement, prisons, and insane asylums are all in place to keep us from causing even more wrack and ruin.

No serious attempt has ever been made to identify a source of our problems and, thereby, remove the commotion at its route because the deepest held belief is that mankind itself *is* the problem. All we have ever tried to do is regulate humanity to minimize the damage.

That, in itself, should tell us there is a deeper problem. It should be apparent in a rather benign universe that all of the disruptions that mankind creates are not necessary. But, somehow, that thought never takes hold. Something has disrupted our existence and, yet, it is no more than a legacy that can easily be removed. Attempting to just keep the genie in the bottle is itself a misdirection, a detour we have followed for millennia.

Would we cause more problems without these legal systems being in place? Certainly. That, though, is the wrong question to ask. The question that needs to be asked is *why do we create so much chaos*? Why are we, in many aspects and instances, acting like an unstable species?

While it is true that it is the way it is, it is not the way it has to be. We are so conditioned to the situation that we never even ask the question, "What's wrong?" The most fundamental questions are never asked. What unsettles mankind? What causes our unreason? Why do we, as a species, act in such an irrational manner?

This is not typical of mankind. Our greatest strengths, due to our sentience, are our awareness, our curiosity, and our ability to ask questions. We question everything. So, *why don't we question the existence of the unreasonable behaviour of mankind?* We turn a blind eye to it. We investigate the phenomena of our aberrations but not the source. The source has been made nearly invisible to our senses through the millennia of conditioning.

Our uneasiness with this intentionally overlooked piece of knowledge has made us avoid a close inspection of the human race itself. That is a very important clue. What is so embarrassing that we always look away? The upheaval caused begins very deep within the fabric of our lives.

Sentience is a complex arrangement that has benefitted humanity in many ways and with which we have created many wonders. It has allowed us to delve deeply into the universe in which we live. It is truly a wonderful adaptation provided by nature.

It also gave us a tremendously beneficial concept that still remains mostly unexplored. A gem of unparalleled brilliance. It is a concept of unrivaled significance, and, yet, it has languished for millennia.

Like the disturbance, this concept appeared very early with the emergence of sentience. Ironically, the two are tied together in many, many ways. The cessation of the disturbance does more than just enable this remarkable concept. The remedy for the disturbance will build a foundation for it.

Unlike the source of our unreason, the gem was created entirely by the celebration of existence. Rather than undermine our existence as the disturbance has done, it has striven to stabilize it, even under the duress of the disturbance. Once unleashed from the fetters of unreason, it will be able to expand to make our lives significant indeed. It has lain nearly nascent for all of these millennia. It has only been hampered and distorted by the source of our unreason.

The two cannot easily coexist. But, since this remarkable concept is not a distortion, since it is not misinformation based on a past mistake regarding humanity's perceptions, it remains like a florescence at the end of the tunnel. It is a sentient truth. It was one of the most insightful creations of all of our existence. It will now be able to flourish unimpeded by our unreason and the root cause of all of our disruption.

Before we consider this most remarkable concept in depth and the achievement of a higher order of existence, though, we must first consider the source of unreason that sent the human race off the rails and how to eliminate it. There is something missing and the gift of unhindered sentience awaits.

The reason for unreason

The most obvious, egregious and insane characteristic of humanity is misogyny. It is a glaring light on the root cause of our problems. It is still just a symptom closely related to the cause, but it is rampant and unequivocally insane.

How can mankind have developed a society in which half of the race has often been treated little better than cattle and seldom, if ever, treated equally? Why would one half of the human population lash out at the other half in such a bizarre way?

This is a very important clue in many ways. Not only does the unreasonable behaviour in this context point directly at the problem but the relative stability of the half that has endured the abuse is also a signpost. Why is one half of the population relatively stable, serene even under the duress of misogyny and other abuses while the other half is bewildered, distracted, whiny, and unreasonably angered to the point of developing an undercurrent that leads directly to misogyny on such a massive, global scale?

Even more to the point is that individual men will often shake their heads at the injustice of it all as if they had nothing to do with the scourge of misogyny. There is only one possible source for misogyny. It cannot be denied, it cannot be avoided. It is men. So, how can individual men act so blameless when it is clear that the male half of humanity is to blame? There is something terribly suspicious in this disparity.

Who is affected the most by unreason? It lies much more in the realm of the man than the woman to cause disruption to our existence. The man, much more than the woman, lead humanity into the realms of unreason. Why is it this has never been recognized or, worse yet, just accepted?

Even more revealing is, why, in a society ruled mostly by men, is sex suppressed? This is a conundrum indeed. Men need sex. They crave sex. Why would men, who have ruled society for millennia, develop a society in which any mention of sex is suppressed so stringently? If you look at the organizations of the past that have made the rules to suppress sex, make it forbidden, or nearly impossible to discuss, they were all ruled by men. Why would men not only tolerate a society in which sex is suppressed but encourage it? Even worse, within that suppressed existence, all forms of bizarre, perverted sexual proclivities are enacted by men. The answer comes closer.

Another oddity is why do men feel the need to be important and in control? Why do men feel so unbalanced, as if their situation were out of control? What lack in the self-image of men makes them seek to feel important and in control? What inferiority complex is being compensated for? What central issue is so out of control for so many men that they have to compensate? There is certainly an over-compensation at work in so many men that it is reflected in the over-control of everything that mankind encounters. It is an irrational attempt to maintain control as compensation for a feeling of complete lack of control and inadequacy in a very important aspect of life.

Why is it that men are so prone to perpetrating domestic violence? It is well-documented that globally the overwhelming victims of domestic violence are women and, also, that they generally experience more severe forms of domestic violence. This does not even take into account verbal abuse. What drives so many men to verbally or physically abuse the one that they supposedly love? What enrages them so, and more importantly, why is it directed at the woman in their lives? The ones that they supposedly love?

Another important indication of what is wrong is the transformation, sometimes radical, that a man's personality can take with a woman once she has been bedded. The bright, happy man can transform, sometimes quickly, into something much less attractive, morose and seemingly haunted. Why is that? There are also the men that bed a woman once and, then, disappear from her life. Why is that? The reasons and excuses, so far suggested, do not even come close to explaining the situation. The idea that the guy is just a jerk doesn't explain anything at all. Jerk or not, he just bedded a woman and should expect that it can happen again. Why would he run from that? Men don't easily or rationally walk away from such a situation including sex. Something is missing. Something haunts this man. Big, *big* clue.

The existence of misogyny is so pervasive as to make one wonder. It is clearly some angst on the men's part and it is on a global scale. It is the widespread sentiment that begins with domestic violence. It reflects all of the violence of mankind, which is overwhelmingly a man's characteristic. The instigator of misogyny cannot even be questioned. It is men. It is verifiably insane. Misogyny makes no sense on a cultural level. The disruption caused by misogyny benefits no one. It is as if men wish to blame women for something. There has to be a concrete reason for it and it needs to be eliminated in a hurry. Humanity have suffered long enough. All of it needs to end.

Why is it that men go through a mid-life crisis? The usual excuse that the body is changing is not very realistic. Another oft quoted excuse is that their lives do not feel complete. No indication, though, of what would complete it. These are often extremely successful men that feel that something is missing. Puzzling indeed. It is the nail. The only surprising aspect of this is that we could blind ourselves so effectively to the answer for so long.

In all of this, we have conspired to cause men, women and thus, all of humanity, to suffer unnecessarily for millennia.

That often-dreaded talk between man and son. Why is it dreaded? Is it that there is something uncomfortable, something awkward? Something that is not said? Something missing? What could be awkward about the most stunning part of existence provided by nature? Why should it be uncomfortable? What is missing?

Some thinking suggests that sentience drove us crazy. That the reason for our unreason is sentience itself and there is nothing that can be done about it. Fait accompli. That, somehow, being more aware of our surroundings has driven us to unreason. Or, even more vaguely, that mankind is somehow just evil. Again, Fait accompli, done deal. Forget about it.

So, we throw up our hands in despair and accept the inevitable. It is accepted like a gordian knot that cannot be undone. Actually, it was the abrogation and intentional distortion of our awareness by our most ancient ancestors, due to an apparently unanswerable conundrum, that drove us to unreason and caused our calamity. It is the results of a flawed sentience.

The gordian knot *can* be undone. Sentience; true, undismayed sentience is a blessing, not a curse. The primary problem is that sentience allows us to perceive - or *misperceive* - our surroundings to a degree that has never before been attained by any other animal. If something of serious significance is misperceived, then there is a problem and our sentience is disrupted. We are deceived. The whole process of deception begins. In this particular case, we have been deceiving ourselves throughout all of our history.

In our past, we made a mistake. We misperceived something that is so central to our existence that our sentience became distorted. It haunts us on a daily basis and never let's us alone. It leaves our lives riddled with uncertainly, bewilderment, anger, and despair.

We now have the intelligence to identify and remedy the problem. Our sentient nature has finally made the problem evident and the beautifully elegant remedy apparent. The remedy was empowered by the desperate need for resolution and the progression of knowledge and intelligence of the human race. In other words, mankind's innate capabilities are finally coming to the fore. This book contains both the identification *and* the remediation of this ancient scourge.

The root cause of our problems is something that wears away at the self-respect of many men and it is breathtakingly simple to resolve. It compromises the self-respect of enough men so that it becomes humanity's problem.

Men have a problem. It is not what we suspect. And, it is dead easy to fix. Let us see exactly what it was that threw mankind off the track of sanity and reason and how to get back on track.

<u>Men have a problem</u>

When thinking that men have a problem and are the leading disruptive force within the human race there is usually one suspect. It is that men are driven to sex and by sex. We stop there and throw up our hands. If it is just the desire by men for sex that causes all of the chaos, what can possibly be done? It is not just the desire for sex.

The real problem is much worse, as well as more convoluted and insidious than that, *but also much more easily remedied.* It is an unexpected, and yet, very common, very well known, very understated problem and it hides in plain sight.

It is believed that all of the quirky behaviours that are predominantly the domain of men are due to a high sexual drive and testosterone. This couldn't be more wrong. The coldness; the anger; the inability to embrace emotions; the rage; the violence; the ruthlessness; the childishness; the underhanded behaviours; the lack of sympathy, compassion, and empathy; the sometimes near maniacal need for control; the false facades of 'manliness'; and the waning of dignity, integrity, and honour are not due to the incessant need for sex, nor is it something that should be expected as a man ages. The real surprise lies in the fact that this excuse is so much more acceptable to men than the actual problem that they have fought desperately - since the beginnings of sentience - to deceive themselves as well as everyone around them. Another huge clue.

The most often accepted suggestion is that the problems of mankind are nature at its worst, that nature made a mistake with sentience. It is actually nature at its finest. Nature was fully prepared for sentience. Mankind was not. For more than three thousand years, we have continued to act like a dumb animal, a brute, unable to embrace our sentience, due to our impeded awareness of something disturbing in our existence. We were just too embarrassed to face it and, instead, accepted it as unresolvable. Huge mistake.

A man loses one critical characteristic before all of those terrible behaviours begin to develop. None of the aberrant, unfortunate behaviours that are so common in men can develop without first losing one's self-respect. The root cause of our problems is the most common reason for the loss of self-respect among men. It is common enough that it infects a large portion of the male population, thus affecting mankind as a whole. Once a man's self-respect is corrupted, any other offensive behaviour can be expected. What could cause a man to completely lose all respect for himself and leave so little emotional control that suppressed emotion is the usual result?

If one really thinks this through instead of just accepting the common notion that sexual drive is the problem, it is clear that sexual drive is not enough to cause these behaviours in men. That does not explain the man that walks away from a woman after their first bout with sex. It does not explain the mid-life crisis. It is only suggested because it is the most obvious distinguishing difference between men and women and the fact that the actual cause is so very embarrassing to a man. Make no mistake, men, there is no reason for the embarrassment or the continuation of the bane on your existence.

The sexual drive of the man is the blatant difference between men and women and, of course, is due to the sperm build up in men that needs release. This drives men to seek release regularly. Because it is such a distinguishing difference, it makes a perfect scapegoat in the place of the terribly embarrassing root cause of the disturbance that runs roughshod over men.

Men's unrelenting drive for sex is not the root cause but it is a determining factor in the development of the bizarre behaviours and situation that develops. Even the quandary of lack of sex for a man only points in the right direction.

In most cases, men have mates. If most men have mates, why would so many be sexually frustrated? *That* is a huge clue. Why is it that so very many marriages end up with separate beds, separate lives, little or no sex, and lots of frustration? That certainly is not what one would expect from such a pleasurable experience.

There is another very important difference between men and women. The more subtle difference is that the man, by the strictures of our existence, is responsible for the sexual satisfaction of his mate. His own sexual satisfaction is almost invariably guaranteed by nature's primary intent.

There is another clue in that long list of deranged characteristics of men: violence, especially towards women that permeates all levels of global society. If you don't believe that men are generally deranged towards women then explain misogyny, an extremely insidious, somewhat subtle, completely insane and pervasive form of violence that makes zero sense at a cultural level.

What is it that drives men to treat the other half of humanity so despicably? Because they need sex? Not even remotely likely. If anything, the reprehensible behaviour of misogyny and other forms of violence towards women is conducive to getting **less** sex and less enjoyable sex from women. So, that does not answer. Men may be brutes, due to the root cause, but they are not stupid.

This clue is so very overwhelming. Men abuse women, even though the obviously smarter tactic to attain sex and a peaceful, satisfying home life is to cherish women and make them wish for more sex. Topsy-turvy, right? Now why would that be? Why would women be disinterested in sex?

What is missing? **The sexual satisfaction of the woman**. Why is it missing? The **completely unnecessary** sexual inadequacy of the man.

Just to reiterate a few points. Learning to sexually satisfy a woman during coitus is dead easy and explained later, so don't let it worry you. If this affects you, do not feel disturbed or alone. It is a great many men, maybe most men and the answer is embarrassingly simple to achieve satisfying coitus for the woman.

Just connect the dots. Many men can't get sex as often as they would like from women. What could possibly lead to women becoming disinterested in sex with men? Only one reason: it is not very pleasurable for them.

If women are treated similar to a bedpost (or a sock?) when it comes to sex, why would they be interested? Women are often just a by-stander for the pleasure of the man with little expectation of pleasure of their own. Make no mistake (it is certain that no man alive that has this problem makes this mistake in his most honest, un-deluded thinking), it is not the woman's fault. She can have just as much pleasure as the man. She can enjoy and desire sex just as much as the man. The only ones who have been truly deluded into thinking otherwise are many women.

Another huge misinterpretation of the situation is to believe that the man has no interest in sexually satisfying his woman. This is an easy conclusion, since a man may often state as much to soothe their own ego. It is a deception. It is easier for the man to state that he doesn't care to satisfy his woman than to admit that he *cannot* satisfy his woman. Or, in the case of the 'one and done' or 'love them and leave them' approach, it is easier to just never face the facts. In repetition to assuage any growing concerns to turn away as this is read, *this does not need to be the case*. Learning to sexually satisfy a woman during intercourse is dead easy and explained later.

The estimates range from thirty percent to ninety percent of men cannot last long enough to satisfy their woman regularly, if at all. The most valid estimate seems to be around seventy-five percent. This was from a survey of women. Even thirty percent is a huge number far exceeding any plague that mankind has ever endured.

It is worth reiterating that there is absolutely no reason for men's lack other than our inability to scrutinize the problem. The answer to men's ability to last long enough to satisfy their woman is detailed later in the book. In short, real men don't twerk. While it takes more than just lasting long enough, it is this lack that drives all of the other behaviours that impede the man's ability to provide the woman's pleasure. It is the foundation of all of our unrest and bewilderment concerning our behaviour.

It is almost surprising that women did not discover this long ago. It seems very likely that Simone de Beauvoir understood the problem to some extent (see the quote at the beginning of the book). But, women are hobbled from understanding the full extent of the disorientation, frustration, and feelings of inferiority that a man may encounter since a woman never experiences anything similar to the lack. Maybe the closest they could ever come to understanding it is to put it in the context of feeling that they have not done right by their child.

The dilemma, the disturbance, that has been plaguing and haunting mankind throughout the ages is that many men have not learned to control their climax at all. It is his responsibility to last long enough to bring his mate to climax but it seemed impossible. If he claims it is not his responsibility, then he is only fooling himself and only consciously. Deep inside, he knows better. Our sentience cannot be denied without causing upheaval, which is exactly what we have endured for millennia. But, it can be deceived. Men need to pleasure women sexually for any hope of a lifetime of great sex, copacetic relationships, emotional stability, as well as sanity. When it is enough men that endure the lack, the same is true for the human race. The implications are vast. It is time for this to end and it is dead easy to last long enough, face to face in a loving tangle.

Men begin to feel unmanly and lose their self-respect if they cannot satisfy their woman. They also lose this most wonderful sexual experience. No matter how gentlemanly, courteous the man is, without a satisfying experience in the bed, his own satisfaction is compromised as well as the woman's. His days of frequent sex are numbered and his sanity is eroded on a daily basis, whether he has sex or not.

When a man is not good at sex, he will begin to question his manhood. Nowadays, at least alternatives, like cunnilingus, are becoming acceptable which certainly has helped the situation. But, still, the feeling persists that a man should be able to do better and it is true. Nature has provided for a sentient species to overcome the lack that is present in most non-sentient animals.

Once the self-respect is corrupted, then any inhuman behaviour can be expected. The initiation of the ability to deceive is almost certainly due to this disruption. The man has little recourse other than to deceive himself as best he can for as long as he can about his lack, thus opening the door to deception and disorder as a way of life.

Do you think that sexual incompetence might be so embarrassing that an individual might want to hide from it? Would it irreparably bend his consciousness? What happens when a significant portion of the world's population is affected by this debility, *especially when they believe it is their own, individual trouble only, not shared by a huge portion of the male population*? By the most viable estimations, it is the norm, not the exception. A man feeling feeble, unmanly has to be one of the most disruptive forces possible. The need for sex *and* the failure at sex are the man's problem. The disturbance is only compounded by lack of sex. It sets humanity up for complete failure as a sentient race. Nature has provided an elegant solution to this disruption of a sentient species, which we will get to in a little while. Sex can last as long as necessary. Nature was prepared, we were not.

The desire for sexual release for a man is viewed as overwhelming which, to a great extent, it is. This is where the argument usually ends. That alone is not enough to disrupt a man's stability. The actual reason for men's derangement is terribly personal and embarrassing, making it almost impossible for any man to accept, much less elucidate. So, the man walks around with this burden for his whole life thinking he is unusual in this respect. The lack eventually leads to less sex which just compounds the problem, the frustration and derangement.

We have never accepted just how common the problem of male sexual inadequacy is. Our conditioning has made us hide from it in every way possible. Thus, it feels like a very personal problem rather than the gender wide plague that it is. It is startling, once it is recognized, just how obviously it is a common problem and, yet, we still have hidden from it. This shows the level of conditioning that has developed over the millennia.

Worse yet, it has seemed insurmountable, which it is not. There are books proclaiming that, if you can't keep it up, get used to it. It's never going to get better. That is not at all true but typical of the approach to the problem to date. The simplicity of the solution provided by nature is truly brilliant. All it takes is use of a rudimentary brain to overcome the issue, once the solution has been identified.

It was never nature's intent to make sex satisfying for both participants of the lower orders of animals. That was not, and could not be, the goal. There is one and only one goal for brutish animals: at any cost, propagate the species, impregnate the female. Strict rules were required for the un-thinking, brutish species. It is, though, nature's intent that an intelligent, sapient race should be able to overcome this obstacle in a most exquisite manner. It is ridiculously easy.

Up until this point in time, we have done everything we can to emulate the lower orders of animals. There are dictates from our past that state sex should only be for the purpose of impregnating the female. Welcome to the lower orders of the animal kingdom and the brute approach to life.

Do you begin to see the stunning magnificence that sentience can be, as well as the confusion that has reigned? It is so much more than a heightened awareness. It is so much more than overcoming the necessarily brutish ways of our animal ancestors. It is a completion of the combination of the male and the female entities. This has always been termed love. For purposes of this book, at least, it will be called Sentient love. This is the remarkable concept that sentience also brought into existence in tandem with the realization that there was something missing in the sexual experience. Sentient love has languished in the annals of humanity's existence, never being able to develop fully.

Mankind is different than all the other animals or can be. Right now, the distinguishing difference is a corrupted sentience, a straddling of the line between our animal origins and our sentient nature.

Mankind recognizes the lack of sexual completion because mankind is sentient. There is just no avoiding that conclusion for a sentient being. It is why our dimwitted ancestors put so many strictures in place concerning sex. They were attempting to continue in the supposed bliss of non-sentience. But, sentience is not something that can be put aside. It cannot be placed in the pantry and taken out only when it seems beneficial. Our ancestors didn't have an answer to the problem, so rules and concepts were put in place to deal with the devastating consequences of not having the wit to resolve the issue of an unsatisfying sexual encounter.

Different societies used different rules and concepts but the results have always been the same, a brutish, animalistic approach that, without fail, caused the women and all of society, as well our very nature, to suffer. We have clung to our brutish origins unsuspecting that nature had provided the solution for a sentient form of sex.

Our bovine ancestors could not find the simple, elegant solution that nature provided because they were way too close to our brutish origins and their sentience had not yet developed. Mimicking our animal ancestors, men have continued to pursue their own satisfaction and their mate's satisfaction becomes of little or no importance. The conditioning, the inertia of paradigms, is what has kept it going so long burying the problem deeper and deeper.

It is likely that, initially, before sentience really took hold, their dim minds couldn't even grasp the concept of their mate's satisfaction. We had just barely evolved beyond our more brutish animal ancestry. As the ruminations began, any suggestions by anyone that it should be otherwise were probably shouted down as forbidden knowledge, the apple, our sentience and knowledge causing problems.

The awareness of the lack was never consciously accepted due to the unfounded despair of ever attaining that goal of sexual pleasure for both. It was deemed impossible. That is terribly sad in that nature did provide an elegant, unbelievably simple solution that extends a man's performance allowing him to pleasure his mate in the most beautiful, natural, sentient, loving form of face to face sexual intercourse while both are looking into the adoring eyes of the other.

Very many men cannot last long enough to satisfy their woman. If you are one of those, first realize that you are not alone. That is the first relief. It is a *great many men* that are just like you. Many, many men are dissatisfied with their performance. In all likelihood, it is a *very* large majority of men that are unsatisfied with their performance.

Poor sexual performance doesn't sound like a big deal, right? It is often joked about in televisions shows and movies, nowadays. It is so accepted that no one even suspects how devastating, at both a personal *and* cultural level, this is.

The lack of pleasuring the mate and the drive for sex creates a real, ongoing, persistent dilemma for a sentient male (i.e. a human male). It has life-long consequences that become a problem because men, unlike other animals, recognizes this lack. It haunts him for a lifetime. It is a problem for all of society and mankind when it is some significant portion of the men that endure this problem, as it is today. There is, really, only one perfect solution.

The man's constant need for sex is a constant reminder that he is a failure at one of the most essential parts of life and what should certainly be one of the most enjoyable aspects of life: the mutual sexual satisfaction of he and his mate.

It is the perfect setup to unhinge a man. He constantly needs sex and constantly fails utterly. In other words, it is a constant bewildering burden that distracts from rational thought, self-respect and confidence, and enables unreason.

The feelings of warmth and comfort from the loving touch of a woman fall by the wayside and just exacerbates the shame and utter frustration. Any feelings of comfort, loving, and joy are completely devastated for the man by the failure to perform as he knows he certainly should be able to perform adequately.

The floodgates of disrespect and shame for himself are opened. All forms of aberrancy and obsession become irrationally justified as part and parcel of a miserable life in which it is impossible to keep the woman enthusiastically sexually interested. Thus, the burden is amplified as his life progresses. The obsession with sex is enabled by the drive for sex without the success. The pursuit of substitute obsessions becomes a common distraction. The aberrancies multiply. Successful sexual congress eliminates all of the obsessive tendencies.

Many women are often concerned with feelings of closeness. It is, of course, the rational view taken by the more rational gender that may, now, be shared by men. Women never suspect that the lack of closeness, the frozen emotional state, on the man's part is due to feelings of shame due to his inability to bring his woman the same pleasure as himself. It is a baffling, bewildering, and disastrous situation. The usual assumption is that he is just not getting enough sex.

Even worse is the case of the man who has learned, probably imprinted from a father figure, not to even consider his wife's pleasure; thus encasing himself in an armour of emotionlessness, reverting to his animal origins and lack of sentience. In all cases, the emotional stability and facilities to reason becomes distorted.

The reactions to this dilemma are almost as varied as the number of men that are plagued by this problem. But, at the center, it is always the same. A lack of self-respect and some form of reaction for the lack.

Men, being part of a sentient race, recognize and care about their lack in sexual performance. It is unavoidable for a sentient male. It is not a forbidden thought. It is an inevitable thought. The real answer is the resolution to this problem which men have been maniacally suppressing since we first gained any real level of sentience.

It seems most likely that this applies to almost any man, at least, to some extent. He may last long enough to bring some semblance of pleasure to his woman, but that that is likely a struggle (popularity of the very expensive little blue pill, the endless web pages on how to last longer are just a couple of examples from a very long list of evidence concerning how pervasive the problem really is) in almost every case. Every man has to fight find a way to last long enough to just keep his woman interested. Unless it is won through the solution that nature intended it can have even worse effects. The Marquis de Sade comes to mind.

This bane explains so much of the behaviour of men. It explains why men are so diffident or belligerent or domineering or violent towards women. It explains why misogyny exists. It explains why men become so unhinged compared to women. It explains why men, unlike women, are not as fond of sharing secrets. There's one secret that no man wants to share. It explains why men seem to remain a bit distant from each other, and often, even their loved ones. They are never certain whether they are unusual in their lack. It also explains why so many men try so desperately to prove their manhood in the most ridiculous and aberrant manners. Concerning the most essential essence of their manhood, it is not only threatened but destroyed. The compensations often border on the ridiculous.

If it were just a few men, the problems, the unreason would never have developed into a cultural distortion. Misogyny wouldn't exist. The rest of the men would have looked at any attempts to downgrade women to cattle with horror. Domestic violence would not be tolerated. Because it is so pervasive, we have endured millennia of some terrible undercurrents. Digging ourselves out of that hole is easily done. It starts with men learning how a sentient male can last as long as necessary during normal sexual intercourse and becomes an avalanche of awakening for the species in its wake.

Hidden problem

The way in which the suppression of this dilemma came about is thoroughly astounding, but also, thoroughly understandable. A man is bad at sex. He has no idea if any other man has the same problem. He is surely not going to ask the question. He will tend to believe that only he has the problem or, at least, question whether his lack is normal. He may even consciously question his manhood, but make no mistake, he will at least question it subconsciously. It is certainly not a problem that he is going to discuss with other men. Instead, many men will go out of their way to show just how manly they are in a variety of ways from completely foolish to completely obsessive to completely aberrant to completely accepting this devastating failure. All the man knows is that he is bad at sex and he does not want anyone else to know it. Many, many other men also have the problem and also don't want to reveal it. Even in the home, in the family, it is rare for a couple to engage in this discussion. In the past, it was unheard of, forbidden knowledge and all that.

Any proposal created by any man that made the problem seem to disappear, to suppress the slightest mention of the problem, or reinforce the man's domination has always been enthusiastically endorsed by many, many men with a sigh of relief. Thus, our problems began.

Can you see how misogyny is a foregone conclusion? The irritating, ever-present problem will always seek an outlet. Women are the perfect target in this instance. A man can't be frustrated with other men due to his lack, especially if he has to consider that other men may not have his problem. He already feels disadvantaged in that interaction.

The end result of all of this, from a woman's point of view, is that women came as close to the status of slaves or animals as possible, from which they are still struggling to reach the status of equality. Lately, one proposal has been for the privilege of joining the sad, deranged "world of men". If you can't beat them, join them. The arguments, the fallacies in all of this are nearly endless. The topsy-turvy world begins to full tilt.

The questions are so numerous concerning the odd behaviours of mankind that there is a whole sub-chapter on many of the questions of inconsistency concerning mankind. All of the questions, when taken together, lead unerringly to the answer that men's poor performance at sex is a serious problem.

Why is it that many men go to sleep directly after having sex? They can't face the truth of their failure. It is just better to go to sleep and not think about it. The thought will have moved to the back of the mind by morning. Why do people often hide in the dark during sex? Men can't face the reality of their failure.

Why do many men only have one night stands? They can't face the woman that they *know* they disappointed (though, ironically, she may not feel that way). This will come as a complete surprise to a lot of women. The man who loves and leaves is just considered cruel and heartless. No woman ever seems to even consider just how bad the sex was. It seems that it is such a common occurrence that they just expect it. Some women are quite content with minimal pleasure and don't even conceive that there is any problem of significance or that it could possibly be expected to get better. The only men with this difficulty that come close to keeping their sanity are those that realize that a woman that doesn't expect to be satisfied is the best (current) solution, as sad as that is.

The main driving characteristic of sex for the woman has always been bearing children. This is not meant to say that women cannot enjoy sex, just that they are mostly driven to sex by the desire of bearing children as men are driven by the requirement of release of the buildup of semen. Nature also only made it a requirement that men achieve orgasm and, hence, sexual release. It is a necessity for procreation. The millennia of lack of satisfaction for women may also have filled women with the expectation of disappointment concerning sexual pleasure. In the modern world, even the desire to bear children is breaking down, adding to the upheaval of the sexual situation.

Let's call this form of undeveloped sexual interaction, that is so very often the case today, non-sentient sex. Sex in which we are acting more like animals than humans. It is a founding behaviour for continuance of the existence of all of the other animal-like behaviours of mankind to which we continually regress. Maybe not the only behaviour that leads to our animal-like regression but almost certainly the most significant one.

Everyone suffers when sex is not brought to a sentient level. It's just that the form of suffering and deprivation varies vastly from one gender to the other. Can you imagine (you don't really need to, do you?) being a person that so desires three outcomes from sex: their mate's satisfaction, their mate's touch, and their own satisfaction, and can only have two? Can you see how the deprivation of one versus the other desire makes all the difference in the world and reflects so perfectly the difference between the two genders? The magnitude of the destructive force behind this small inconsistency in life that has crashed through every aspect of human life for millennia. It is time to pick up the debris, rebuild the foundation, and move on.

A great deal of the disturbance to the human condition is related to this failure. Much of the disillusion and disruption of the human race is nothing more than men trying to hide from the world and themselves the embarrassment of the most devastating failure of a life event. For a woman, it is trying to understand why her mate changes so radically for the worst over a lifetime. She will certainly wonder why the act of sex is so appallingly unworthy of the effort, thus leading to her eventual lack of interest; thus leading to the unending downward spiral of what should have been the couple's copacetic, blissful relationship.

The disturbance continues to erode the relationship and the emotional stability of humanity. Remember, it is a continuous failure that grinds over and over, again, ad nauseum, throughout a lifetime because of the man's constant desire for sex and inability to make it an attractive prospect for the woman. It is like the ultimate carousel of nightmares. Repeated over and over, again, until something finally breaks. The ripples outward into the rest of society's behaviour are endless.

Only a brute that has been pummeled throughout his lifetime could think that this is the way it should be. Disappointment and failure are not the required calling card of sentient life.

Do you really wonder why men go through mid-life crisis? In retrospect of this insight, it is very straightforward. How can a man, a sentient being that senses this lack, feel like a man if he cannot satisfy his mate? It becomes completely emasculating as it seeps slowly into his awareness throughout his lifetime reaching an intolerability near mid-life. It proliferates into all of his behaviours; distorting the man's world view, and, thus, disrupting all of human life.

Real men don't twerk

To put the solution most simply, real men don't twerk until the Lady sings, but the woman should twerk to her heart's content. This is the most important insight concerning a man's ability to sustain an erection, though there is much more to an intelligent approach that is described in detail in the chapter on Techniques and Considerations. Interesting, isn't it? Once again, completely topsy-turvy. Men do the twerking, and it is the rare woman that is so bold, since it only accelerates the man's loss of control.

There is not a man alive that doesn't crave to hear the sounds of his woman's complete satisfaction and his woman begging him to let it end. They can now both have the immense satisfaction of those final deep plunges when it makes sense. Instead, today, most men have to be content with a "thank you" or an unconvincing "that was great" and are lucky if they get a sympathetic moan of any proportion (think Meg Ryan, "When Harry met Sally"...).

There is also essentially zero doubt that this almost ridiculously simple change in technique, will work for any man with more intelligence than a bedpost, unless he is incapacitated in some way or are not willing to apply the effort to learn to satisfy their mate. The keylog blocking the flow of reason can now be removed. It was essential to get to the understanding of what it takes for a man to last.   Just discovering the root cause of our unrest would not remove the keylog. It would only have exacerbated the situation.

It is appalling, really, just how simple the answer is for a man to last as long as his muscles don't give out. If our ancestors hadn't striven so very hard to bury the problem, to suppress it through deranged conditioning, it could have been solved millennia ago.   It would not have bent our existence out of all proportion into a caricature of sentient existence. Historical forces, though, are slow to erode and new insights are even slower to overcome past obstacles. Especially when any mention of the subject matter is completely repressed due to fear.

Real men don't twerk until the beautiful woman sings is a lyrical way of putting it. While it is a little more complicated than that simple statement makes it seem, that is the essence of the necessary change for a man to perform adequately, feel like a man, embrace his manhood, and end the destructive tendencies that mankind has engaged in for millennia.   It is all about an understanding of how the muscles and glands involved in sex interact and it really is as simple as a sunrise. The key insight is to stop the ejaculation process in its tracks before it ever begins rather than just delay the inevitable once it begins. Better yet is if the woman does twerk during the whole event, making sure her clitoris is stimulated. This was, of course, abnegated for the woman in the past because it would only bring the man to climax even more quickly. That will no longer be the case.

Let's take a quick survey. All men that can last as long as he pleases during coitus without ridiculous struggles, if you feel satisfied with your sexual performance, please raise your hand. All women that have men that last as long as she desires, please raise your hand. Yeah, didn't think so.

It's been a slow process to overcome the barriers, the conditioning, imposed in the distant past to recognize this lack and do something about it. It has been impeded by all of the conditioning and customs that have been handed down to us.

Disturbances and distortions

The fact that anyone can now have good sex is the tiniest fraction of what this is about. This chapter details a number of the disturbances and distortions that mankind will no longer need to endure.

The distortions that can be fairly directly tied to non-sentient sex in a sentient race are many. Misogyny, domestic abuse, and deceit have already been mentioned. There are more that link almost as directly. Are there other factors at work to distort humanity's rational approach to life? Not any that could affect our views on life as significantly as a disrupted sexual situation. What can be more disrupting to humanity's existence than distortions involving sex, the most fundamental reason that we exist and will continue to do so? It is an activity that is desired on nearly a daily basis for decades. It is a perfect example of Pavlov's dog's indoctrination when the activity is radically disturbed. Our sentience will not be denied. To portray sex as bad or something that should not be enjoyed is just a surrender and return to our animalistic origins that can never work and is silly even to contemplate.

Nature made sex in a certain way to assure the continuation of the species and provide an accelerated form of evolution. That was enough for non-sentient animals. They needed to engage in sex for the sake of procreation with no distractions. An overwhelming mechanism to keep the proliferation of a dumb animal on track was in order. Worry about the mates satisfaction? Not likely.

Mankind, on the other hand, needs to make sex work for a sentient race, a race that has enough awareness in its head to realize that sex is not as good as it should be, could be. That conclusion for a sentient race is unavoidable. It is only the difficulty at arriving at a solution and the repeated failure at really making it work elegantly that has continued to immerse the men in unreasonable behaviour.

The Dalai Llama has noted how, even in the midst of plenty portrayed by advanced western civilization, the misery was quite apparent. The source that has baffled mankind is finally overwhelmingly apparent. It is time it is removed.

The tide has now turned. We can become truly sentient and pursue that remarkable quality that will bring us an enlightened view of existence. But, don't hold your breath, and don't despair. It won't happen overnight. The many distortions and disturbances that mankind has endured will take a long time to unravel. We need to put every effort into doing so but the change required is radical. It will happen but it will take some time. Once the impetus to avalanche of unreason subsides, it will take some time for all of the rubble and boulders to settle.

Distortions

The issue of non-sentient sex seems so obscure that we don't even consider it when viewing all of the seemingly complicated problems of mankind. The type of problem that is easily identified as a result of non-sentient sex are those that seem to indicate unreason and a bewildered animal's approach to life.

It is extremely difficult to accept that such a small change could have such a huge impact on human life, but the ripple effect of this incongruity, this bewilderment to our thought processes are nearly endless. Sentient sex would allow human life to flow much more smoothly. Will all of our troubles disappear? Not likely. How much impact can be expected? A great deal. The phrase perception is reality describes the situation well.

Beneath it all, the nagging thought persists that something is wrong. If one looks at today's society, it is easy to see the distrust of nearly everything concerning society and humanity itself.

We rail against everything, never pointing the finger where it belongs, thus confusing the issue further. We point at the differences between individuals, societies, governments, religions, etc. We point at the systems of man, the institutions of man, the greed of man, the society of man, the leaders of man, the news, the horrors, the insanities, the wars, and the corruption. These are all just symptoms. The primary scapegoat is that man is just a broken model due to his sentience. The goal has always been to just minimize the damage while hiding that which is disturbing our sentient nature. In this context, the faulty, creative logic that was used to mask the real situation is more than apparent.

These finger-pointing reactions so confound because they never address the central issue. It just remains as an uncomfortable knowledge that something is wrong and the invalid assumption that there is nothing that can be done about it. That it must just be endured.

The acceptance of behaviours on the part of modern society that are less than acceptable is due to the continuing distorted nature of our existence due to sexual disruption. Every step forward is paired with a step back. Balance is missing.

What would be reprehensible behaviours in an undistorted sentient race, are deemed acceptable because they are so common. In all societies, disturbing behaviours are frowned upon but accepted as inevitable.

This is also representative of the nature of the problem. Disturbing behaviours do not need to be regulated by outside forces. Frowning and legislating can never resolve the issues completely. They need to be eliminated at the source, the individual. They need to never develop. The individual himself must see the behaviour as reprehensible. More exactly, he must never have any instigation that develops the behaviour.

To arrive at the true state of being human, including unobstructed sentience, sentient love, and something that resembles sapience we must finally break through. We must finally shed all the thoughts that we are nothing more than another common animal that is sorely deranged and needs to be contained. To put all of that finally behind us, this root cause of unreason must be recognized and addressed so that the distortions never develop. Let's look at all of the damage that is tied directly or is closely coupled to a failed sexual model for a sentient race.

Guilt and self-image

All of the aberrancies of mankind can be traced back to a distorted and disturbed self-image of so many individuals that it shows as a dominant characteristic of the race itself.

The self-image always desperately attempts to mask or adjust any reflection that is not complimentary. The first reaction to a faulty, emasculated self-image is an increasing loss of self-respect. There is certain to be some desperate attempt to repair the self-image in some way. The sometimes ludicrous portrayals of manliness are just such a compensation technique. This cannot help but encourage the loss of self-respect as the subconscious recognizes the compensation as self-deceit. Deceit has its first instantiation. This leads to guilt, shame, confusion, enablement of ulterior motives, and further disruption of the self-image. These are not characteristics or circumstances that encourage clear thinking, sentience, or sapience.

A broken self-image leads to distorted perceptions that create a world that is more of a dystopia that it has any reason to be. It creates a distorted view of existence. The distorted perception becomes the primary reality for all of society when it is shared by enough of the population. The broken self-image leads to the destruction of self-respect. Men have a nearly completely broken self-image when faced with sexual inadequacy. The link to the overabundance of violence, cruelty, greed, and so many more negative aspects of the human condition is direct. There is no doubt that the ramifications of sexual ineptness on behaviour are significant. There is no doubt that the number of men that have been inept is large. Larger than any plague that mankind has ever encountered. It becomes clear that our unreason is not a natural state. It is induced.

The beginnings of the reemergence of honor, integrity, courtesy, and the realization that mankind can transcend its past will be indications that we have finally gotten on the right path. These characteristics, today, are considered pipe dreams. Why is it that mankind can accept dystopian concepts so much more easily than utopian concepts? Because it is all we have seen to date. It is not being suggested that we are about to enter utopia, just that anything resembling the current disturbed way in which we exist is not required. It is just that a truly sentient existence, in contrast, may seem like utopia in comparison.

Self-destruction

Is it any wonder that there are a number of people that are driven to self-destructive tendencies? Even as children, surrounded by adults, they often have had despondency, frustration, distrust, and deceit built into the very fabric of their lives. It is easy to understand how feelings of self-destruction can accrue.

That people are willing to strap bombs to their body and blow themselves up, in the context of non-sentient sex, is not even surprising. It is just the ultimate example that life without sexual adequacy can generate despair of the highest order. Life can be considered worthless. All it takes is a little encouragement in the face of non-sentient sex in the form of some further minor disruption or encouragement by role models or authoritarian figures. This is especially for the young that are completely blind-sided by the emergence of sexual inadequacy in their lives, their lives already turned upside down by the subconsciously acknowledged failure at sexual adeptness. It is so similar to the story of Jekyll and Hyde as to make one pause.

Many stories have been documented lately of the nice young man that transformed into a monster that was willing to blow himself up. Note that many of the ones that are convinced by their elders, embittered by their own lack, to strap bombs to their bodies are in that stage of post-pubescence when sexual inadequacy can be expected to come crashing home. It has become clear that it is not so much any particular cause that is necessary as the fact that some young men are seeking an outlet for their desire for destruction. If life is lacking in other ways, then the will to self-destruction can easily reach the tipping point with little encouragement in the presence of sexual inadequacy. Being immersed in a society that seems foreign in its nature can be just such an impetus. If the injustice of it all becomes perceived as overwhelming than self-destruction can seem a viable answer. Remove the single impediment of non-sentient sex and the whole structure of self-destruction begins to fall apart. No need for seven virgins in the afterlife when you can have good sex in this life.

Malice and vexation

What vexes a man? It seems a lot of things do, but really, there is an underlying cause that makes the minor upsets become amplified beyond all reason. It is a grating at the very center of an individual's existence. What instigation can really drive a man to extremes, to serve out malice in prodigious portions? There's only one that can overturn a man's sanity (other than just the total upheaval of his life through happenstance, an unusual enough occurrence) and that is inadequate sex, which also leads to inadequate amounts of sex, whether in a long term relationship or not. This only adds to the frustration and leads to the corruption of reason.

Unreason has been unleashed for as long as mankind has been attempting sentience. To further the argument that non-sentient sex is the culprit, keep in mind that the male of the species is far more prone to all of these aberrations. What else would distinguish one gender as more prone to aberrations?

Mid-life crisis

A man is born, and throughout his adult life he regrets one thing subconsciously and it blindsides him when he reaches his mid-life. It builds over a lifetime at a subconscious level, slowly seeping into some level of his consciousness.

Can there be any doubt of the source of mid-life crisis? What else, other than a disappointing sex life, could cause a person that seems successful in all other aspects of life to become so distraught as to throw away everything as they reach middle age? Like a pouting child, the man finally realizes that all is not as it seems. Life and its celebration turns completely to ashes. It is not a sudden occurrence, it is a slow burning pressure cooker than finally explodes. It is a final acceptance of the awareness that has been there all along that all is not as it should be. A man might very well have been completely successful throughout his whole life, and yet, when he reaches middle age, the nagging suspicion that something was never quite right comes home to roost and he is willing to throw it all away because the most important aspect of life, sentient sex, has never been achieved.

Look at the characteristics of a man's mid-life crisis and it becomes very, very clear. He does everything he can to regain his youth and show off his wealth if he has it. It is not just age. It is not some fear of the approaching end. A person that is satisfied with one's life would not yearn to throw it all away and start over. The man strives for an image that will attract women. Sporty cars, sporty image all are the normal route of mid-life crisis (not to even mention that many men's whole lives from the time of pubescence are cluttered with irrational ways in which to attract a female).

Everything he has done in a lifetime begins to pall. None of it was fulfilling without the completion provided by satisfying sex. He is attempting to fill that gaping hole in his life. Without the ability to pleasure a woman, he will continue to fail to fill that gaping hole. It is a mad attempt to try to do it all over, again, and get it right. His consciousness still hasn't accepted or confronted his failure and he is at a loss. Until that failure is confronted and overcome, there will be no resolution.

Most men go through the delusion, subconsciously, that non-sentient sex is something that will magically disappear with age or experience or, when they find the right woman. It is a blind, desperate, non-sentient hope. These are the rationalizations, self-deceits that are developed because no real answer is apparent. When they reach middle age, they can no longer sustain the fantasy. They know they have failed, over and over again, at the most important aspects of life, pleasing their woman. Even at this point, it remains mostly a subconscious realization. The blatant characteristics of the mid-life crisis make the source clear.

How can a man ever openly admit, even to himself, that he is terrible at sex? It ends up as a vague feeling of lack of accomplishment, a feeling that life is not complete. That something is missing. Men go searching for completion still embedded in the delusions that it is not them. It is a carousel that can't be exited without the complete, open realization of the source and resolution of the problem.

Domestic violence

Domestic violence is all about obliterating feelings of emasculation, an insane way to show just how manly they really are. They are futile attempts to ruthlessly suppress the reality of the situation. Another unending carousel of disappointment.

How is it that some men, clearly men that have become completely unhinged, are willing to brutalize the woman that they, supposedly, love and refuse her escape from the situation and their control? Their inability to sexually please a woman is the inescapable conclusion. They consider something so embarrassing and disturbing that they will go to severe lengths to hide it. Society is so embarrassed by it that it will not admit it, will not react, even though it is blatantly obvious. The conditioning maintains its hold. The men desire a manly self-image that does not continually distort into feelings of failure. They desire to continue to have sex as regularly as they please, no matter how bad the sex is.

Non-sentient sex is surely the primary cause of domestic violence. The desperate and violent attempt to assure regular sexual release and continue the unsuccessful attempt to remake the completely corrupted self-image into something that is respectable to oneself and, therefore, others. The combination of unsuccessful attempts at sexual competency and ongoing corrupted self-image just continues to exacerbate the situation. Threats or beatings are used to scare the woman into submission or redress his manhood. Can you not see the emasculation in all of this? These kinds of traits make men lesser creatures than even the common animals of the planet.

Think of a man who subconsciously knows he is not good at sex, and yet, he feels he deserves sex. He knows he can't please the woman, so there is no way that he can expect the woman to continue to be interested. Domination and intimidation are easy cards to play for a man, especially if he desires to stay with one woman (going through women like water is another alternative used by many, especially those with enough money to do so. Just as craven but, maybe, less violent if the distorted self-image doesn't cause too many problems and the Marquis de Sade does not emerge). He may also, subconsciously, blame the woman. That she is not reaching climax soon enough.

If that went away, if he knew how to last long enough during intercourse, then he could feel confident in romancing the woman into being interested rather than dominating her into submission. He could, thus, maintain his self-respect. Of course, she would be willing if it wasn't just a futile exercise on her part. If sex was satisfying for the woman, it would be simple indeed to interest her. He would have a whole self-respecting image that would include dignity and integrity. Violence, verbal or physical, domination, intimidation and subjugation would not become part of his character.

The true prevalence of this problem is not acknowledged. The fact is that this disturbance is much, much more prevalent than humanity is willing to admit. When verbal violence is added to the category, it is a surety that domestic violence is far more pervasive than anyone is will concede. It is worth noting that this behaviour is present throughout all strata of society.

While this may seem the extreme case, it is far from it. The Marquis de Sade and the whole idea of embraced sadism comes closer to that distinction. The ways that men have invented to obliterate feelings of emasculation are numerous and heinous. Rape, the sex trade, child abuse of both sexes, slavery, and other more accepted forms of subjugation, all have the taint of a sexually inadequate man's distorted thought processes. The taint is of a man aberrantly attempting to redeem his failed masculinity in the most aberrant, perverse forms possible. It is a sickness at the heart of mankind and can be easily remedied. A man that is confident in his sexual ability will have zero desire to dominate and coerce.

One of the saddest, appalling, and most horrifying aspects is that many women are instilled with a guilt complex, convinced that she deserves this treatment. She may have been taught to believe that it is all her fault. In a world in which very few men can satisfy, this is a very easy conclusion for the woman to accept, especially when the man (or her father or both) is telling her so. After enough experiences with more than one man that is inept at sex, it would seem to make sense that it is her fault, her flaw. Does it need to be mentioned that it is not her fault?

Misogyny

The worst curse that mankind has inflicted on itself is misogyny. What could possibly cause a race to treat one half of its population reprehensibly? What could possibly justify the treatment of one gender as little more than cattle? There is no benefit but only disadvantages to such a distorted relationship. It is so counter-productive that it is clear that there has to be a furtive source for the disruption of what would otherwise be a positive, celebrated, and beneficial relationship between the two sexes.

Domestic abuse is the beginnings of this ripple effect. Misogyny is the end result. Inept sex is the cause of both. What other source of disturbance could really cause the delusion that required one gender to make itself feel more important and wish to subjugate the other? What could be so lacking in the masculine self-image that they had to elevate themselves in such an artificial, disruptive, counter-productive manner?

It is certainly not a natural state to disrupt what should be an egalitarian relationship of interdependence. What angst could possibly be wearing away at men to make them feel the need to suppress women? What is it about the situation that can make men feel so threatened and insecure that they need to ensure women are treated as slaves and assure that they have little to say concerning the workings of the world? A woman that is self-assured and confident in life (which is more natural for a woman undisturbed by feelings of sexual inadequacy) certainly grates against a man's already emasculated self-image. To assure that this doesn't happen required subjugation, a second class position.

This is the biggest disaster of blind-sided sentience and sexual debility. What makes it so incredibly ludicrous is that men suppressed those that were never the source of the problem but always and in all ways the victim. What makes it so incredulous is the millennia of conditioning. The victimization of women developed for no other reason than that men's manhood *felt* threatened. The feelings of emasculation required a scapegoat. The greatest fear was that women would finally realize men's ineptness at sex. Call it the grand embarrassment, if you like. That weakness of seeking a scapegoat is also repeated in many other aspects of life. Just like deceit, it is enabled by the bane of sexual dysfunction and moves on.

Misogyny is really just the more general case of domestic violence. It is the same sentiment as it fans out from the home into society. It is the view that started in the home but became common throughout society. In both cases, it is much more prevalent than modern man is willing to admit. Men have been attempting to beat women into submission in the face of the seemingly impossible task of eliminating the source of the problem. Beatings is not an exaggeration in far too many cases, now or in the past.

The ineptness at sex of the father is reflected in the actions of the boy child and explains the often seen young boy's attitude toward young girls and peers. The way that young boys treat young girls to get their attention is often harsh and disparaging. Of course, they want to get the girl's attention because they like them. Isn't it odd that the emotional reaction that they have learned to replicate is harshness rather than caring?

Where and why would they have possibly picked up this bias? In most ways, it is exactly the same as bullying, and in fact, is the most obvious source for the genesis of bullying. It is misogyny and the desperate attempt to seem manly in the face of feelings of emasculation handed down from father to son that begins to be amplified once puberty is reached.

Things have become so distorted that it is now not unusual to find bullies of both genders. Do not let that fool you into believing that the cause is other than non-sentient sex. Do not fall prey to the belief that it is just the stronger taking advantage of the weaker. It is the ongoing ripple effect of non-sentient sex moving farther and farther afield. It is just brute behaviour of a distorted sentient race. It is just the steady progression of the disturbance as the rituals and strictures of the past fall away and all of the angst and anxiety due to the frustrations taking the form of viciousness.

If men felt confident in their ability to build fully functioning relationships with women none of this would occur. There is something fundamentally wrong when the situation between men and women is undermined through every step of the process of the relationships.

That it starts at the very roots of the individual relationship and ripples outward into every facet of that relationship and all of the interactions at every level of society is no surprise. Young men, never having been taught the single most critical necessity of a physically loving relationship and, instead, are inculcated with the despair of the father and founder at their first attempts at engaging the opposite gender. The breakdown of the insupportable, irrational strictures of the past just amplifies the problem. Worse yet, the model set down by the distorted behaviours of their sexually incompetent father lets the disturbance begin even earlier in life. Thus, the behaviours take on new, more creative malice with each generation as the full extent of the lack becomes increasingly apparent throughout a lifetime. The justifications and rationales become more convincing due to early instatement before the critical thinking develops.

Those first steps, when a young man is attempting to discover how to deal with the opposite gender in a general way in the face of the disturbance of non-sentient sex, are the foundations of misogyny. The characteristics become fixed once puberty and sexual engagement cement the disappointment and emasculation. The general sentiments of character already in place from role models, followed by the first experiences of inept sex, grow to become the disturbance in society's relationship between the two genders.

The scapegoat for the man's feelings of emasculation in the presence of the individual woman grow in scope to encompass all of womankind. Over the many, many generations that have preceded over the many millennia, the disturbed individual relationships evolved into the globally spanning misogyny. The disturbed personal, individual relationship slowly evolved, due to the need for a scapegoat and the unsuspecting feminine gender suffered. The necessary rationalizations to justify the excuses and finger-pointing, came to such a state that it finally began to emerge as a template for relationships of one gender to the other.

Does this surprise you concerning a bunch of folks that began as little more than apes with regards to knowledge and understanding? Does it surprise you that a bunch of knuckle-dragging primitives made, at least, one big mistake? Is it not the expected outcome? Any high regard we have for our ancestors is misplaced.

The conclusion, when perceived in context of non-sentient sex, is obvious. All of the suppression and hostility towards women in the many varied forms across all cultures, throughout history, certainly stem from the lies and the unresolved, unperceived, irrationally justified, and subconsciously recognized sexual inadequacy of men and the perceived threat to their masculinity.

Not only is improvement of male sexual stamina important to our sanity. It is also important to women being finally accepted as equal citizens without all of the undercurrents, distortions and clamour of all of society and both genders presently in vogue in the effort to achieve that equality.

The concept that legislation and enforcement are needed so that women can be accepted as equals is maybe the most fundamentally ludicrous and infuriating aspect of all of the ridiculous distortions due to non-sentient sex, highlighting the topsy-turvy nature of our current existence. It is the perfect example of attacking the surface issue with no regard for the source. It can never provide the natural equality that is required. Misogyny diminishes humanity. It reinforces the belief that mankind is inherently broken. Women, in desperation, have attempted this liberation as is most understandable. Men need to quickly take the real step towards providing that unshackled equality by first freeing themselves of their own shackles of emasculation.

The endless contortions that the disturbance has put mankind through over the millennia are mind-boggling and saddening. What is all of the nonsense about the woman being the temptress except an excuse for poor behaviour on the part of the man, brought on by his ineptness at sex. Yes, she is just dying to not be satisfied.

While women are finally demanding their rights, they should be embracing the cherishing, love and respect of all of society. Anything less is a travesty. Women should not be scraping to get respect, they should be adored without condition. Misogyny points to the root cause of our unreason as accurately as a magnet points to metal. It is an important indicator of the sexual frustration of men brought on by non-sentient sex.

The inability of the man to please his woman, physically, has been a disaster of unmatched proportions.

Sociopathy and misanthropy

What could cause a man to become so insensitive as to treat all of mankind without compassion? It happens when one's own self-respect is so crushed that one's honor, dignity, and integrity no longer matters because they are lost. The burden of sexual inadequacy is just such a phenomenon.

Other men are viewed as a threat to an emasculated self-image. True camaraderie at any level becomes a facade of competition. Distrust of one's fellow man is just one of many ways in which a man deals with his threatened self-image.

If one feels at a disadvantage, that person can easily decide that any advantage taken in a situation is reasonable once the self-respect is compromised. This distortion is the backbone of sociopathy. In the case of feelings of sexual inadequacy, it is a defense mechanism against the faulty situation in which the man feels unfairly disadvantaged or threatened. Stabbing others in the back to achieve a prominent position by relegating all others to a mental image of less importance as a human being is an all too common scenario. These self-serving behaviours are a hallmark of non-sentient sex. Empathy is lost. Sociopathy is substituted. The man also will begin to feel some compensatory level of superiority in place of the satisfying feelings from knowing his manhood is in tact. It is that false manliness, once again.

Many other inducements may chip away at the humanity of men but this is a fundamental, essential, and substantial aspect of the problem. The threatened self-image and manhood and fear of disadvantage precludes any possibility of overcoming inducements towards sociopathy.

Misanthropy, like misogyny, is, much more common than conditioning allows us to recognize. We are so immersed in the characteristics that we take it for granted. It's not considered misanthropy because it is just the way it is. Nodding our heads at the horrific headlines is none other than misanthropy. "Mankind is so screwed up." Is that other than misanthropy? This is a common viewpoint in our world today. The sentiment is mentioned in many articles headlining the news. It is again a form of compensation. "You see, it not just me!"

It is truly strange when considered. Many today will tell you that mankind is pretty screwed up, but in the same breath, they will tell you that their close friends are great people. Humanity is screwed up but the people in close contact are not? It's just that the disruption is best recognized at a distance and in the mass reactions rather than individuals in close contact and on their best or suitable or compatible behaviour, where the disruption may not be evident in close one on one relationships. Another example of Jekyll and Hyde. Just as the anonymous comments on many web pages bring out Mr. Hyde. Road rage is a similar situation.

The institutions and systems of man certainly allow for and, even encourage, sociopathic and misanthropic behaviours but they are not the driving factor. It comes down to the people, always. Rationalization and self-deceit are the vehicles. The systems are one of the road on which it travels, but disturbed people are at the heart of the problem. They are the drivers and they are driven, themselves, by the disturbance that is non-sentient sex and the loss of self-respect.

The institutional structure used by most organizations can encourage an already faulty self-image to care less and less for one's fellow man with respect to one's own success and the manipulation of the people and the institutional structure for one's own advantage. This is only encouraging an existing tendency, though. The initial impetus to consider oneself so lacking in any form of self-respect as to make the corruption something that can even be considered is required There has to be an entry point for the insensitive behaviour to even begin.

What provides a person that initial degradation of self-image and loss of self-respect? What leads a man to respect himself so little that he can treat others with even less respect? By now, it should be obvious.

Deceit

Is it so hard to believe that humans are not deceitful by nature? All of the self-serving, destructive deceit of mankind has an initiation into existence at the individual level. A source, a substantive reason exists for the continued corruption of our sincerity at the individual level. It is also reinforced when it encounters collaborative efforts. In other words, the endurance of deceit over the ages has made deceit acceptable because it has become common practice. In the absence of the initial self-deceit of the individual, the characteristic of deceit has no reason to develop in the individual and would wane quickly within the human race.

It is an abhorrent characteristic that seems likely to develop only when self-esteem has already been thoroughly corrupted. It takes a towering force to overcome our natural tendency towards truth. That is why court systems work to some extent. When under the scrutiny of our peers, it is a horrible, unnatural feeling to deceive. Most everyone has the urge to truth.

We act as if deceit is a natural occurrence. There is no reason to believe that. Every indication is that we despise lying in ourselves. Once someone truly embraces lying, his character becomes unhinged. There is no reference for the belief that deceit is a natural occurrence.

Rationalizations become acceptable in the face of the original, compelling self-deceit that disorients the character. Deceit can, then, take on a life of its own based on the original development of unreason and deceit due to non-sentient sex. While deceit may seem common, natural, and unavoidable, just remember, like all of the other traits of unreason, the scourge of sexual ineptitude has had millennia in which to have its way with humanity.

The trait of deceit is generated during each individual's lifetime. There is an original impetus towards the trait of deceit. Maybe the only unavoidable instance of deceit in a man's life is that which is incurred as a way to cope with the disturbing realization that his masculinity may be in question. It is initially a way to hide this realization from oneself in an attempt to hide it from the world.

The self-deceit incurred due to non-sentient sex has been engulfing humanity in deceit for millennia. Non-sentient sex in a sentient race is a perfect fit for all of the parameters concerning the emergence of deceit. The desperate struggle across all strata of society to hide something too embarrassing to bear is certain.

The invention of lying. The original source of deceit occurred when sentience collided with an unfortunate pre-existing condition that could not be faced by mankind. More specifically, each man in his despair would use one of a variety of rationalizations to deceive *himself* concerning the problem of sex that he could not conquer. Deceit of oneself and all of society was required to hide the fact that men are terrible at sexual intercourse, as a rule, because no resolution was apparent.

Once deceit is adopted by an individual, it will easily proliferate through many, if not all, aspects of that person's life. The barrier has been broken as the self-image becomes damaged and self-esteem is undone. Will any lesser force be able to induce an individual to compromise his integrity?

Will pervasive sexual adequacy remove all signs of deceit from the human condition? Humanity's natural state is one of self-respect (i.e. everyone wishes to respect themselves). This drives the desire to remain honourable with integrity, dignity and all of the other positive human qualities in tact. These have to be disrupted by powerful forces before deceit can be considered. They will not easily bow down to lesser forces.

All forms of craven behaviour by humans have had one overwhelming instigator. The forced disorientation due to the conflicting aspects and requirements of the sentient sexual situation overwhelms efforts to retain self-respect. Thus, our honor, dignity, and other redeeming qualities are compromised. There are certainly other corrupting forces that have been developed due to non-sentient sex that may take a long time to ameliorate. Whether there are other, lesser forces that can cripple a man's ability to retain his dignity, especially under duress, remains to be seen. Any much lesser force will not have the pervasive success that non-sentient sex has had.

This, of course, does not include the gentle lie that is told for the sake of honour. The lie that is told to avoid causing another person unnecessary harm or discomfort does not damage one's self-respect. These are not lies of corruption, self-benefit. They are lies of a seemingly beneficial nature. It is difficult to determine, at this point, what role they actually play, and if the gentle lies will also become a relic of our past. Is even the perceived unnecessary harm that induces the gentle lie a relic of non-sentient sex? It is entirely possible.

Honor, dignity, integrity, courtesy are all natural components of our self-image driven by our desire to respect ourselves. They are not something we need to learn or achieve. They are naturally occurring and are torn out of our grasp. Yes, deceit should disappear in, at least, its most dishonourable and virulent form. There are many other forces that are at work to undermine our self-respect but they are all secondary and tertiary effects compared to the driving force of non-sentient sex. Is there any other cause that can force the majority men to deceive themselves; thus starting the whole debacle? It seems unlikely, though a man in desperate straits is another matter entirely. How desperate must a man become to overturn his self-esteem?

Escapism

Mankind's desire for mood-altering substances, such as alcohol, drugs, cigarettes, etc, as well as other forms of escapism, such as the fascination with fantasy in the form of books and games may very well be completely driven by the vast disappointment and disillusionment of life caused by non-sentient sex. The circumstances of life, otherwise, do not answer. The disruption of life is too widespread among the affluent to blame the poor aspects of life among those in more abject situations. One disturbance can account for this desire to escape.

The escapism that whole swaths of humanity indulge in is an escape from a world in which one's own sexual disappointment requires distraction. The most absurd point here is that we do not even attempt to cure the disruption or sexual dysfunction, but instead, we try to cure the minds of those that recognize what a disaster it all is. The goal is to put these people on a drug so that they no longer see what a mess the world is (escapism is self-medication).

The generation that grows up without the plague of non-sentient sex and all of it's unreasonable by-products should have less need for the many, many substances, substitutes, and pursuits that mankind uses to assuage its turmoil. The awareness that was granted us through sentience can finally be a blessing instead of a curse. We can cease hiding from our existence.

Lucidity

In some ways, beneath all of the disturbance and pain that typifies human life today, there always has been an ongoing struggle to make things right, to find a way to fix all of the nonsense of a race that is inadvertently clinging to its animalistic nature. Each time we come to believe that it is just the nature of existence is when we fail utterly. A way in which mankind can finally break out of the trap has always been sought and the lack of the identity of the source has always caused the retrenchment into unreason.

These are the ongoing cycles we see, over time, in our existence. The cycles have been repeated ad nauseum. We swing from a desperate desire and a will to get to the fundamentals of our problems to the acceptance of our faulty existence and surrender to the belief that the human race is little more than a smart, though deranged animal. Continuously, through all of these cycles, we have engaged the surface minutiae with rare attempts to dig deeper.

Most important are the repeatedly failed attempts to really get to the heart of the matter. Even though they have failed, these revolutionary thoughts keep pounding into our consciousness that something is just not right at a fundamental level. Once again, make no mistake these attempts are the results of the gentle, loving hand of the fairer sex. This is the gender that is not overwhelmed. It is not their failure that is disturbing our existence. At some fundamental level, they can sense that the disturbance is not necessary but they can never quite grasp the nature of the disturbance that encumbers men. This is the gender that can more easily comprehend that mankind should be something more. Chivalry and the Flower Power movement are examples at such attempts. It may have failed but it pointed the compass in the generally correct direction.

The list goes on

This is not nearly a definitive or comprehensive list of the disturbances and distortions that mankind endures. It is just the most obvious that tie rather directly to non-sentient sex. It is also a list of the worst of the disturbances to our existence. What must be kept in mind is the ripple effect. These closely tied disturbances are likely enough to overturn any shred of sanity in the human race and lead to many of the other disturbing qualities of mankind when a significant part of the population is affected.

Men and women

It is worth noting the stark difference between men and women concerning the behaviours listed in the chapter above. While women cannot be categorically eliminated from displaying any of these behaviours, even misogyny, they are, on the whole, much less prone to the behaviours. They mature better. They can be influenced into these behaviours by their social environment, but unlike men, it is not their most inherent behaviour. They are not affected by the personal failure that leads to the loss of self-respect.

Not the end of world hunger

Sentient sex is not going to end world hunger, poverty, war, economic upheaval or many of the other myriad problems that face mankind. Maybe though, unencumbered by the delusions, distractions, obsession, aberrations, disappointment and rage that are the hallmarks of the era of non-sentient sex, humanity can finally overcome these issues. What should surely be expected in a race that finally has respect for itself is that all of mankind should be able to begin to raise itself and all of its members from the muck. Do not think this is only speaking of the materially unfortunate of our race. It is speaking as certainly about many affluent that are mired in the muck of material, as well as, other obsessions.

Sentience and Sapience

If life is about anything, it is about the relationships between people. What happens if the most important relationship between two people is disrupted for the great many? That single relationship that engages the physical senses more than any other has been disrupted since the very beginning of sentience. It is a disruption of the most fundamental relationship on which humanity itself and all of its cultures rely and it is disrupted on the physical level.

Sex, in most cases, is still as non-sentient as the apes. The contravening existence of our sentience in the face of animal-like sex causes a disruption that rocks those relationships at their very foundations. It *is* Pandora's box, it *is* the apple. It cannot be put back into the box. That is what has always been attempted up to this point. That is attempting to dumb down the human race to brute status which we have done superlatively. We must move forward and now we can. That shred of hope at the bottom of the box was all we ever needed. It is time for humanity to overcome its heritage and grow fully into its gift of sentience.

So far, only bewilderment persists concerning the subject of sex. It is the one topic that never gets discussed openly. It is the subject that has blocked our attempts at an unimpeded sentience. Everything about sex, the one reason for existence and something that should be celebrated, is hidden in dark corners.

Sentience is the ability to perceive one's surroundings to an extent never before attained. It is an excruciatingly definitive awareness of one's surroundings that desperately needs to have a clear, undistorted view to function properly. It is a complicated concept that goes far beyond detecting one's immediate physical surroundings. Any animal senses their physical surroundings, and in some simple manner, is aware of those surroundings with regards to itself. Mankind has an awareness at a heightened level, especially with regards to oneself in the context of one's surroundings and interactions.

We have engaged our sentience, our awareness, in so many ways, driven by our natural curiosity. Due to that curiosity, we have delved deep into the workings of the universe from size and scope of the larger inhabitants, such as stars, galaxies, and local groups to the tiniest most insubstantial particles, such as quarks and wavicles. We have delved into the oceans and life on this planet and all of existence. We are investigating whether life forms exist outside of our planet. No, there is nothing wrong with our sentience when it is applied. It is when our sentience is bewildered and blocked that we suffer.

Because we have avoided scrutinizing sex, it has led humanity to avoid scrutinizing itself. We do not look at the human race itself in a sentient manner because we can't tolerate the scrutiny that comes to bear on our sexual dilemma.

We look at everything in context of ourselves ... except ourselves. We are bewildered. We shrug our shoulders concerning all of the disturbing characteristics that disrupt the current scope of human existence. "That's just the way it is, so deal with it" is the mantra. Bad mantra. Brutish mantra. A mantra developed in the face of a seemingly unresolvable dilemma.

This has been our idea, so far, as to making our desperate way forward: put a lid on our unreason rather than eliminate it. It is clear that we, somehow, have convinced ourselves that unreason is our lot in life. That a sentient race that expresses something so terrible is not wholly functional.

Sentience is a relatively new gift, with respect to life on Earth, that mankind needs to finally, fully embrace and can do so once we have put away the single most distorting lens to that sentience. Becoming comfortable with our sexual nature will finally let all of the pent up frustrations and stupidities that have burdened mankind over the millennia dissipate. We will be able to embrace our sentience, put away our childhood, and finally move forward. We can regain our balance.

In most ways, the human race became completely sentient many thousands of years ago. We embraced our sentience in almost every way, except for sex and humanity itself. Unconstrained sentience does not require a complete overhaul of the human race. It just requires that we become sentient concerning *all* subjects, including and especially sex and the human race itself.

In every other matter, we seem to have shed the nonsense of our forefathers. It's just that the implications of sexual disruption are so far reaching. It is so central to our existence that it implicates everything concerning the individual's existence and function. It is only full awareness of what is really occurring within the human race that will allow our sentience to become fully functional. The last frontier is mankind itself.

Because we are sentient beings, deep inside us, we realize that it is not the way it should be. It is that inherent honestly once again. We are aware that we should be able to transform sex into love, but there has been something missing. A deep-seated fear and belief by men that it was an insurmountable problem has caused havoc for millennia. We have hidden in fear of failure to overcome the problem. This has also made it impossible for mankind to inspect itself closely and find that the fear is unfounded. Sex and mankind itself, the most important topics for us to understand thoroughly, have laid languishing while we made great discoveries and breakthroughs in every other field. Instead, rather than a close inspection, we threw up a blind of conditioning, laws, enforcement, and the assumption that sentience inherently brought about some delirium that had to be contained. In retrospect, it is almost unbelievable.

Very often, nonsensical explanations are put forth and accepted in desperation to explain whatever we fail to really understand. This is tremendously significant in anything we consider, but *especially*, when it comes to sex. Sentient sex is a cornerstone of unimpaired sentience, and with that attained, a bewilderment is removed from the human race. The distracting, pesky fly of non-sentient sex will no longer buzz around and within our heads. It is to be expected that nonsensical answers to all concerns will not be as easily accepted within an emotionally stable race. Non-sentient sex is far more disastrous than thinking that the universe rotates around our planet. If we can't inspect our own nature, then we can't expect to ever fully embrace our sentience or achieve sapience. Critical thinking is critically handicapped.

We can become a stable, thoughtful, powerfully endowed race that can take on any problem once we become an integrated whole, unburdened by disillusionment and deception. This will allow our complete harmony with our sentient existence. As we cross pubescence, it should slowly become an awakening into maturity. Is it any wonder men have been incapable of maturing in the current state?

How does a species make that transition into sapience? To keep the two words straight, sentience is awareness (how aware could we have been not to recognize that our sex is lacking and terribly disrupting our existence?). Sapience is wisdom. A strict definition of sentience is the ability to perceive, feel, or experience subjectively, or in the context of oneself with regards to one's surrounding. A strict definition of sapience is the ability to think and act using knowledge, experience, understanding, common sense, *and* insight.

When the sentience of an individual is forced to accept an unrealistic view of the world due to conditioning, it is crippled, the awareness becomes distorted. When the sentience of enough individuals is crippled, then the race is crippled, as well. There is no chance of sapience under such conditions. Sapience isn't even a remote afterthought. It is thrown out and replaced with misconceptions, deceptions and self-serving, scurrilous behaviour that worsens as the sentience state becomes more fully developed. Sentience is hampered and sapience remains nothing more than a distant, vague concept until the obstacle is overcome.

Sex is essential to existence for the human race and demanded from a biological standpoint. The clash with sentience was inevitable, there was no avoiding it. Sex is far too intimate and important to the self-image not to have devastating consequences when it is non-sentient sex performed by a sentient being. The issue has to be resolved for the species to rectify the path of existence.

Could mankind lead a lot more stable, sentient, sapient, satisfying life without this impediment? Ya think?

There is a phrase a woman that is adored once mentioned that says (paraphrasing) 200 years from now there will still be sex, love, death, and violence. Sex, death, and violence, up until this point have been a certainty. Existence of love, up until this point, has been compromised and questionable. While the concept of love has existed for millennia, the achievement of the reality has been constrained, at best. The continuing existence of violence now comes into question and the prospect of the much broader definition of sentient love dazzles the horizon. Sex, and death are the most likely to continue to exist. The remarkable concept of love should finally takes its rightful place. It is the most important concept that mankind ever developed. Or, more exactly and almost certainly, womankind developed. Violence may be virtually eliminated.

We might just be able to eliminate violence or, at least the vast majority of it. When there is violence in the home, as there is today in inordinate proportions, then it will ripple out from there into all aspects of life. The rage, aggressiveness, and combative tendencies, in large part, are a by-product of our disrupted sexual expression. Eliminating the source of the vast majority of violence in the home will ripple throughout the rest of humanity's existence like a ray of light, as well.

For the man, as the bewilderment recedes, the clarity of the situation and the celebration of having an unfettered sentience will begin. As the men begin to achieve the same sentience as the women have always possessed, the women will find their footing, as well.

What could be considered the most sentient form of sex? Following nature's lead to a fine degree, only digressing for the sake of hearing that lovely sound of satisfaction from your lady's lips, is the ideal: face-to-face in a loving tangle. Most other sexual inventions are just a remnant of non-sentient sex. Nature knows what it is doing, it just required us to have the wit to realize it.

We need to accept that sentience changed everything. We can't hide from it. We cannot return to our brute origins, though we have tried that for millennia. It wasn't sentience but clinging to our animal origins in the sexual arena that caused the majority of our disorientation. The last few millennia are a testimony to that. The chaos that has reigned since we first emerged as a tentatively sentient race makes it clear that accepting a significant non-sentient element within a sentient framework cannot succeed. It just upsets the balance.

The potential for brute violence amplified by the ongoing growth of knowledge and wit of sentient existence is a dangerous combination. The more dangerous the weapons that our creative minds develop, the more dangerous the situation in the hands of an unbalanced race. It remains to be seen but the preponderance of interest in developing weapons may even wane. Until we understand this universe a great deal better than we currently do, it may suit us to continue to create weapons as long as we don't continue to feel the need to point them at each other. That startling possibility seems at least within the realms of possibility within a truly sentient, sapient race.

It is worth considering, also, that the possibility is this. That sapience, as much as goodness, is the natural birthright of a truly sentient race. It only fails when the sentience is impeded, blocked from the natural progression.

Just begin to imagine what a relief it will be when one can have satisfying sex and multiply that by some large percentage of the population of humanity and you will begin to recognize just how significant a change this could be for humanity. It should bring a stability to the species unimagined up until this point. It is much more than that, of course. It is also the self-assuredness of the individual. It is also all of the qualities attained by having self-respect and an integrated regard for oneself. We will be a lot closer to achieving sentience at that point. Sapience and sentient love should definitely be within our reach, finally. The unimpeded maturity of the individual should lead to the maturity of the human race.

There is a quote that was encountered that says it all. "Love without borders". This book is attempting to make it clear that humanity can find the love that really suits us as individuals and as a race. It's just that the way has been blocked up until this point in time. We need to rid the human race of the most disastrous form of folly that has driven the human race since the beginnings of sentience. This will finally mandate the opportunity for love without borders. We can finally be able to spurn the road of destruction that we have followed for so long.

Imbalances

No sentient race can ever truly succeed without knowing itself. Imbalances will result. Along with our success in other aspects of our existence, the imbalances become more prominent. Our misery, due to the gaping hole in our awareness, has been amplified as the imbalances between material success and emotional atrophy increase.

The imbalances we induce in our environment, society, culture, desires and goals are all just a reflection of the imbalance in our private lives. The wild variances in attitudes, the left versus right, etc are all initiated by this personal imbalance.

The dismantling of unreason

Why does a person become unreasonable and imbalanced? A person that is self-assured in their existence and their daily activities does not as easily fall prey to unreason, deceit, and self-deceit. Someone that is confident in themselves and maintains their self-respect will face everything that is encountered in life with reason, honesty, self-assurance, and a proportionate response.

Life has many hurdles but mankind has proven itself capable of facing any hurdle. If it is faced. Anything that can unhinge the human race, as a whole, must start by unhinging the individual's self-respect, thus undermining the self-image, and it must be a large majority of the individuals to have a significant effect on the whole of the human race. Nothing could do a better job of unhinging the human race than non-sentient sex.

There are so many questions that, especially combined together, reveal the truth. That non-sentient sex is the culprit and sentient sex is the solution becomes obvious. It is a completely different effort to confront this truth and find the remedy. It was an interesting challenge indeed.

We have evolved far from the lower primates and it is time we realized that and distinguished ourselves as human, not just an intelligent, extremely dangerous monkey with a problem. We need to prove we are really sentient and sapient. So far, we have donned the mantles of sentience and sapience without the qualifications. It's like owning a race car and believing, therefore, one is a race car driver. Usually, that ends in a wreck.

Our ability to resolve issues has never been brought to bear on the problem of our unreason until now. The root cause has now been resolved, for all intents and purposes. We no longer need to endure unreason. The dismantling of unreason is in progress as we speak (or read).

Sentience is enabled by intelligence, curiosity, and knowledge. Those factors are all in place and will only become more prominent as we emerge from unreason. Sentience just needed to be unimpeded by delusion. Sapience may take nothing more than a stable environment for a sentient race, as easy as throwing on a cloak. What is being stated here is that mankind is like a tool that has been bent due to misuse and abuse. A tool that could never be truly useful. Its expected functionality incapacitated. Once mankind is unbent, the misuse and abuse ended, it should recover quickly.

In retrospect, the final simplicity of the solution is so very perfect, so very elegant, so very natural and, yet, extraordinary.

Being human

What does being human mean? Sentience is certainly a big part of it. It also, though, involves the effects of already existing conditions on that sentience, such as being descended from animals.

What is profoundly important to understand is that goodness is not something that needs to be learned. The natural state of humanity seems to be goodness. It is crucial to see beneath all of the varied nonsense, conditioning and paradigms that mankind has endured to see the truth. Some of the nonsensical paradigms we tolerate are completely disabling. Beneath all of those layers of nonsense, what is found is that mankind is good due to its natural proclivities.

Goodness, just like sapiences naturally occurring and only fails in the presence of corruption of its essence. Everything we have been taught is directed away from the assumption that mankind is essentially good. Until that assumption is overturned, we cannot delve deeper into our place in the universe. Until the assumption is accepted that mankind is *not* inherently flawed, we can delve no deeper into a true understanding the human race. This will occur naturally in the absence of non-sentient sex, but may be difficult to accept until after the fact.

Interestingly enough, we have focused on the wrong animal traits to base our existence and beliefs concerning what it means to be human. Worse yet, some of them are not even accurate. For instance, did you know that wolf pups and fawns will play together? There is also a tribe of baboons in which the arrogant alpha males were removed through their own arrogance by eating tainted meat that killed them. The tribe survives wonderfully without them and ousts any alpha males attempting to join their group. Also, no new alpha males develop within that tribe.

The suggestion that the genetics of animals makes us ruthless to begin with, is specious and unfounded. Ruthlessness is a learned trait, even in animals. Benevolence seems much more likely to be inherent, only to be lost when corrupted or necessary for survival.

We have a yearning that is surely inherent to be accepted, beneficial, and useful. All humans wish to be of value to their fellow man. If they don't, then it has been conditioned out of them. There are whole subcultures in most parts of the world that have been taught since childhood to never expect to be of value. It is built into most modern economic systems. Full employment, for instance, can never be sustained. So, some fair sized portion of people have been taught to subsist without providing value.

A lot of the assumptions concerning our inherent flaws are just inertia from the miserable conditions from which we emerged and continue to accept. We don't need to drag that baggage with us any longer. That the conditioning has held throughout the ages is like a mantra repeated without cessation and without thought. It is the pitiful acceptance of our disturbed nature as inherent and the willingness to believe that what we see is all there is. A close self-inspection is in order. With the emergence of unhindered sentience and reason, the gaping flaws due to our misperceptions will be apparent and the results of that close inspection will surprise.

Once this hurdle is overcome, the close inspection of other aspects of humanity's situation can begin in earnest. Mankind will know when the time is right.

The human condition

Being human is radically different from the human condition. The current conditions of humanity are still closer to the animal state than the state of a fully developed, sentient, rational race. An intelligent, damaged animal may be the best description of our current state. That is just due to the conditions, not a requirement. Satisfying sex will relieve a lot of our disruptive tendencies.

Sapience seems to be further and further from our grasp if one studies history and current events. The combination of sentience and one critical flaw in our awareness that we allowed to develop resulted in humanity repeatedly returning to brutishness. As our aspirations for greatness of the human spirit are pummeled repeatedly and as we are inundated with the *perceived* actuality of the situation by the mass of information technology, we are finally beginning to accept that condition as fact rather than the distortion of mishap after mishap piling on top of each other. This is the key that was left out of Santayana's pithy statement. It is more than just knowing the past. It is rooting out the instigation to disruption and baring it for what it is.

The point that he should have made is how shocking it is that we repeated everything in such shocking detail. Change the names of the individuals, countries, economies, and governments involved and the same preposterous behaviour is repeated over and over, again. The real point to take away from this is that it is nothing more than madness. Madness invariably has an instigator.

There are much bigger horizons now, so our repeated return to the depths of the brutish state become far more dangerous. If we don't eliminate the root causes of our problems we won't survive as a race. We're not just playing with clubs and axes anymore. We've got some serious capabilities and serious problems nowadays. In the hands of an irrational race, we'll bite the bullet one of these days.

Our condition doesn't need to take the Vulcan way, depicted in Star Trek, of eliminating emotions to get there. That would certainly be a disaster, though Gene Roddenberry's sentiments can be understood. Nor, do we need to develop irrational relief from the scourge of inept sex in the form of alternative lifestyles and pursuits. We just need to understand why the human conditions of emotion and reason are so out of control. We need to become truly human, truly sentient, unfettered by blinders. We need to face what destabilizes our emotions and reason.   A stable emotional environment is what is indicated, achieved by removing the impairment. A far greater level of reason can then be expected.

Overcoming non-sentient sex is an interesting scenario.   It is the first example of sentient evolution.   Intentional, directed improvement of the clarity of sentience for the purpose of a vast improvement in the situation and the chance to finally make a serious attempt at sapience.   It may not be the last.   The purpose is to rid ourselves of some significant portion of our unreason and cluttered awareness in order to peer deeper into the human condition.   The current condition of unruliness and misperception contributes significantly to unreason.   Once the current clutter is removed, we will see what is left.   The development of sentient sex can finally open the way for another sentient concept: love.

Sentience has done nothing, until now, but shine a light on an absurdity concerning an aspect of many non-sentient species' existence, including primates, that just does not function properly for the one sentient race.

The absurdity of our situation has been noted ad nauseum by many. But never addressed until now.   It is represented in many forms of philosophy, theater, art, and political stances that just leave a glaring light on the subject and does little to alleviate it. The constant polarization of mankind into many shards puts further light on the absurdity of it all, though it is seldom recognized as such. Romanticism versus industrialization, existentialism versus religion, conservatives versus liberal, religion versus religion, government versus government, and the list goes on, all in essence describe a lack in mankind and an absurdity about our current condition.   They are all feeble attacks on the surface issues that count for nothing in the grand scheme of things.

Too many things break when a sentient race deceives and confounds itself, until the race itself fails utterly. A sentient race must be able to embrace all aspects of its sentience unfettered.   A sentient race that deceives itself is not sentient. It is only a deceitful race that causes all of its own anxiety. It is ignoring the facts of its condition that causes it to fail.   Until we finally, proudly wear the mantle of sentience and sneer at the concept that it is the cause of our problems we will continue to fail.

In one very important way we were like children that were unaware of our actual condition. We played at life while carrying an unnecessary burden and delusion that no sentient race could ever bear. Full sentience and the burden are mutually exclusive.

With one simple insight, all of this changes. The human race can finally, really celebrate being alive and move on in a much more rational manner. Once we replace our unreason and discontented sex with sentient love, both the physical and emotional aspects will gain drastically in scope and beneficence. This will pour through every aspect of our lives.

The most ludicrous irony of all

Just think of how ludicrous it is. Men are driven to seek sexual release all their lives only to find that they are a failure at making the prospect an engaging topic for their mate. The house of cards is unmatched. A man's manhood fails miserably as does his prospects of having sex as often as he would like. That rampant unreason is the result is not surprising. Is this not the very definition of despair? It is reflected in every thing mankind does.

A woman may or may not be able to gain a sense of this disruption but, be assured, she sees the results. Every man reading this, that has passed puberty without achieving sexual adequacy, clearly understands. Just the freedom from the misconception that it is not an unusual problem for a few individuals will be a vast relief. That it is not an inherent, inescapable failure is far more liberating. It is the first step away from unreason.

One of the mysteries of life is the awkwardness between men and women. Is it any wonder in a race that hasn't a clue about how things should operate between the two genders? Nothing of substance is ever passed on from parent to child with regards to the opposite sex. The best most children can hope for is that the parents are not at each others throats constantly.

A man spends his first post-pubescent years reveling in the wonder of release. How baffling and disappointing it is when the man discovers that he has no basis for understanding how to extend the sexual encounter for the sake of the one with whom he attempts to share his life, love, and pleasure. Is it really a surprise that men become emotional husks? With nowhere to turn to learn the necessary essentials, he is at a loss. How helpless, hopeless and frustrated he begins to feel. All of the worst characteristics of men need not exist at all. Whether it is the false portrayal of masculinity or the withdrawal from life into some form of escapism or obsession or dismay, they all lead back to undeveloped sexual ability.

All of the wonderful expectations of which he has been dreaming in his youth begin to fall to ashes. It may take many years before he can face the perceived, distorted fact that sex will never be good. And even this unfortunate and unnecessary belief may never be faced fully. It may stay a subconscious rumination that never is allowed to enter the conscious mind. Any number of rationales may be adopted to avoid facing this most distressing realization, but in the back of his mind, the man knows that this is not as it should be. The destructive nature of this realization, especially at the subconscious level where it typically lies (double entendre), cannot be overstated.

It is worth repeating. Sexual pleasure can and should match all of those early expectations.

The avalanche

There is no process of logical thought that supports the conclusion that unreason is our natural state. The rationale that it is just a part of sentient existence is not a logical conclusion.

Unreason is not our natural state. It was not inherited. It is just a change in conditions, due to sentience, that needs to be faced and overcome. Overcoming obstacles is the bread and butter of mankind.

Non-sentient sex may seem like an insignificant trifle compared to all of the problems of mankind, but maybe, the best analogy is the pebble that causes the avalanche. If one assumes that unreason is not the required state of mankind, as is certainly the case, then something is causing it. Some, small, distorted, and therefore, unrecognized fact concerning our existence, that goes unnoticed, started the unreason rolling. It is the pebble that enabled the avalanche to pour down the mountain into every aspect of our lives, destroying and disrupting the very basis of our existence along the way. The boulders tumbling down on us are just so obvious that we spend all of our time combatting them, dodging them, never suspecting that a tiny pebble began the avalanche and keeps it going. Non-sentient sex for a sentient human race fits all of the criteria of that pebble.

The destruction won't end just because we finally see it coming but, once the understanding of how to overcome is embraced, it should take relatively little time to begin to subdue the avalanche of unreason. The conquering of that pebble, the crushing underfoot of its existence, will be something fine indeed.

Animal traits

There is no more powerful behavioural mechanism than sexual drive. There is a difference, though, between the mechanism for sexual drive and that for sexual performance. The former is a mechanism driven by biological necessity. The latter is a trait that can only be developed through intelligence and would be a hindrance for the non-sentient sexual lifeforms. They are content with relieving the sexual and biological pressure, and if adequate sexual performance and satisfaction of the mate is not achieved, it really does not affect them. The thought and the edict that sex is bad stems from this conundrum. It is a too simple solution that did nothing to address the actual problem. But much simpler than attempting to solve the problem.

The desire to bring one's partner as much pleasure as oneself is a behavioural mechanism driven by sentience. The desire cannot be denied. Only the fulfillment can. The desire only happens because sentience gifts us with the potential for something more than brutish characteristics. This also highlights a particular aspect of sentience.   Sentient beings naturally have a higher, more complete, order of caring.   It is just the fuller awareness of sentience being applied to caring.   That mankind has such trouble with it just show our disrupted nature.   That women have much less trouble with it, just shows where the problem lies.

This also reinforces the concept that mankind is naturally beneficent and that sentient love is our natural state.   That is, once we are truly sentient in an undisturbed manner.   It will signify the emergence of the evolved concept of caring we call love. It's been there all along waiting patiently for us to evolve, just as the women have been waiting more than patiently for men to evolve.

No other life-form on Earth is sentient to the extent that we are. They are not interested in pleasing their mate.   The males are just interested in sexual relief, the females and nature are only interested in proliferating the species. Fertilization, alone, is the end game of a non-sentient race.

As long as the human male is only achieving sexual release and relief, the human race will remain no more than an animal and a brute.   Due to our sentience, it is a state even less than an animal in some respects. We remain a deranged species, caught somewhere between sentience and non-sentience. Unreason is the hallmark of an unfulfilled sentient race. Caused by that pesky fly of non-sentient sex that distracts us.

Only humans have the awareness at a level to contemplate their mate's onticfaction   The disparity between the two mechanisms, sexual drive and sexual adequacy, is what causes the unreason of mankind.

We know that nature does not always succeed in its attempts. The failed attempts are identified by the end of that race's existence. We will fail if we do not shed our conditioning, accept the obvious, and move on. We will not even have the satisfaction of blaming it on nature. We now know that nature has done its job. It's time for mankind to carry it through (pun intended).

We are too advanced in our steadily increasing awareness of all aspects of existence to continue without evolving our sexual nature.   It is absolutely necessary for us in order to avoid failure as a race due to the destructive aspects of unreason.

Are you sentient or not?

Identity

A man's identity is completely bound up in his sexual being.   It is a primary driver of a man's identity once it emerges at pubescence.   One can easily imagine a woman's complete bafflement when the man she thought she knew so well, that was fun-loving and easy-going, slowly becomes discontented, disgruntled, distant, and morose as he faces his own sexual inadequacy in the face of his lover without discovering how to resolve it or, most often, even admitting the failure consciously. In essence, he begins to become disoriented. His life's learnings have begun to fail and utterly betray him.

There are surely a lot of things at which to point a finger concerning identity crises. Dissatisfaction with work, financial troubles, etc. These minor upsets do not comprise the identity to nearly the extent that sex does. Make no mistake, if a man's identity as a sexual being is assaulted - not by external forces but internal subconscious realizations - his character can change drastically. No other inconvenience can act with the force of non-sentient sex.

Any of the other normally suggested sources of identity crisis are paltry in comparison. They do not really have the power to transform a man's personality to the degree that a continuous, repeated assault on his ability as a lover will impose. This is the primary difference between men and women that is nearly impossible to explain to a woman since she doesn't live through the forces at work in a man. It also explains the dual nature of their serenity compounded with the frustration and/or anger incurred by living in a man's world.

This is also a clear indicator of what makes men and women so different in their views and approaches to life. Throughout the spectrum of human conditions, the woman's character is more stable. Why is it that men, under the same conditions, are so unstable? Testosterone or the burden of being the bread-winner do not really answer. The aberration of inadequate sexual ability does.

A man has a sexual drive that strongly wills him to find release for the pent-up semen. He also desires the soothing feeling of the touch of another human being, just as a woman does. The man's release, alone, is not enough for a human sentient being that has a heightened sense of his surroundings. Especially when the failure will surely lead to less release in the future in the most satisfactory manner. The satisfaction of the partner is essential. Further, any benefit from the soothing feeling of touch is crippled for the man by the failure to provide pleasure in full measure to his mate. The woman takes what little pleasure she can eek out of the situation.

These are a stark differences. The man sees his woman go unsatisfied while he, on the other hand, is completely satiated. The woman sees the man fully satiated while she goes uncompleted. Which one is going to feel guilt? Which is only going to feel hopeless?

From a woman's point of view, the man's situation is extremely difficult to comprehend. If she has never encountered a climax (which happens more often than one may think), she won't even understand any reason for sex other than having children, which is becoming a diminishing requirement in the modern world. The pressure cooker of the man's situation is just as foreign to a woman as air is to a vacuum. Mostly, they just seem to shrug it off as their lot in life. This also is a cruel shame.

She certainly will never experience the pressure from the build-up of semen. A healthy man in his prime should probably have sex, at a minimum, every three days. He probably could have sex every day or more. The man's growing frustration in the absence of sex may seem incomprehensible to the woman.

While regular sex is surely just as healthy, and potentially enjoyable activity for the woman, the overwhelming drive for release of semen is not present for women. With the lack of the extreme sexual pleasure of orgasm due to the man's inability to last, it becomes only a curiosity of some interest to the woman due to biological drive and the vague pleasure involved in the act itself and the soothing touch of another human being. Even the biological drive is being overridden nowadays due to many considerations.

To reiterate, this is not to say that women do not have a drive for sex or the same potential for sexual pleasure. If anything, their potential for sexual pleasure may even be greater than that of men. It is just not an overwhelming urge and orgasm is not a foregone conclusion. Men must learn to last as long as it takes. There must be no limiting factor to the sexual act other than exhaustion.

Even the overwhelming drive of the male does not mean that he will necessarily be obsessed with sex to the exclusion of all else. This only happens in the current case of non-sentient sex, the aftermath of the increasingly limited interest of his partner, and the distortions introduced to his mindset due to failure.

A desperate desire for release can supplant the desire for love with the much simpler requirement of rutting and attempts to recover one's masculinity. The desperation, due to the man's knowledge that he is not satisfying his mate and his mate's growing disdain for something of minimal pleasure, distorts everything concerning the relationship of the man and woman and the act of sex. Rutting with anyone that will accept him becomes the oft-accepted, simple, deranged solution to a situation that seems insurmountable.

Even worse, as is often the case, is when the man doesn't even pause to consider that the few moments of coitus are not satisfying for his partner. Baffling indeed; for both involved. Some men have difficulty comprehending that sexual release for the woman is not the predetermined outcome from sex. Less rigorous thinking will lead him to blame the woman for her lack of satisfaction. The woman that does not understand her mate's regular desire for something that is often only mildly pleasing to her without the release will begin to find reasons to avoid the wasted effort.

So much of all of this never enters the conscious mind because all the inhibitions that have been heaped on everything surrounding the sexual act repress the thoughts. It is just acceptance of a situation that does not need to be accepted. We are smarter than that.

Men's widespread repressed concern about sexual incompetency that has gone unacknowledged causes a massive inferiority complex that has held men in thrall throughout the ages with increasingly damaging compensation behaviours that affect, not only those men, but causes machinations throughout the workings of society. The disruptive ramifications of this for the human race cannot be overstated. They are nearly endless.

All of the swagger, all of the desperate desires for men to seem manly are bound up in feelings of inferiority and emasculation. It distorts everything about the masculine mystique. Manly replaces masculine and can be defined as distorted in most cultures. In others, the compensation will take different forms. In all, they result in an undercurrent of misogyny. These compensation techniques that are faulty by the very nature of their existence, cripple the race and the individual's life and those around him. This failure to feel adequate at life has taken its toll on the entire human race, its history, its society, and its decisions.

Today's entertainment vehicles don't help at all. Entertainment, such as popular fiction, movies and TV shows, often portray some men as being naturally gifted, and also, showing so many supposedly sexually satisfied partners that the clear assumption is that most couples are sexually satisfied. The comic relief is usually some man who is portrayed as incompetent with women; thus incompetent at sex and life. Both characters make their characteristics seem inherent, as well. It is this disturbing image that is inaccurately etched into the mind of society.

The other assumption that arises from this is that there are a great number of men that are sexually adequate. There is no evidence at all to support this, outside of fiction.

This is so misleading as to convince most men that there is something wrong with only them and that nothing will ever help. That they are an outlier. They sadly accept the situation and the unacknowledged psychological damage done. Multiply that by hundreds of millions of men, if not billions and you will begin to get the picture.

Of course, in the not-too-distant past, it was radically different. It was nearly impossible to even ask a question on the subject of sex or find any reference to the subject. This was a double edged sword. The cultural rituals and rights made for a race that just had to "accept the inevitable" and made the lack as palatable as possible, which contained the problem to some extent. It also created a false order to our existence. The animalistic traits were reinforced. Sapience and full sentience were set aside. The disturbances of non-sentient sex can never be completely contained. They can only be finally erased by sentient sex becoming the norm.

The traditional terms used to greet the bride and the groom, in western societies, are revealing. A groom is greeted with, "Congratulation". The bride is greeted with, "Best wishes". Interesting, that.

Men are taught to be "men" as compensation for the inability to be human due to the failure at a most fundamental aspect of their existence. Masculinity and femininity are valid concepts. There are certainly real differences between men and women but, there are more similarities. Should caring, compassion, tenderness, and kindness be an almost exclusive quality for one gender or should it be a human quality? The man's characteristics have been blown completely out of proportion, resembling a caricature instead, due to the distortions of non-sentient sex.

The self-image of the man has been making a desperate attempt to find resolution from the emasculating realization of sexually inadequacy in all the wrong ways. The current definition of being a "man", at least in the U.S., is mysterious indeed. "In charge" may be the least offensive definition that can be suggested. Callous and insensitive is a better description, especially when it reaches the point of violence, either verbal or physical. Suppression, hidden emasculation, feelings of inferiority, and disruption of emotional value are the most accurate terms to describe it.

One rather global phenomenon in the last few hundred years, shared by cultures across the world that had little contact with each other, was the attempt to rise above our ignoble past by encouraging such behaviours and attitudes as honor, integrity, duty, courtesy, and respect (all being behaviours that are consistent with sentient love), often in tandem with monarchies. Chivalry, if you will. This was a significant, if troubled, attribute of monarchies. Those who ruled, those with power over vast numbers of other humans, were at least superficially taught the importance of dignity, honour, etc. To quote from The Story of Roland, "To deal justly with both friend and foe; to be courteous and obliging to his equals; to be large-hearted and kind to those beneath him in rank; and above all, to help the needy, to protect the weak, and to respect and venerate the ladies."

This was a desperate attempt to force the qualities of sentient love into men that are so abundantly present in women. It didn't work very well. The ravages to the man's psychological makeup are not so easily repaired.

These qualities were mostly aspirations and seldom reality. They were finally crushed under the boot of non-sentient sex. The two cannot coexist. The dream of humanity becoming more than a grubbing animal that had been pushed to the forefront of existence, lasted only a short while. As it waned in crushing defeat by the unseen specter of non-sentient sex, it came to be considered a quaint concept that had no place in reality.

Once again, we accepted that we are no more than a deranged, parasitic animal that needs to have its unreason contained. The higher qualities of mankind's existence will only reemerge in the presence of sentient sex.

All of these admirable qualities, encompassed by sentient love, are qualities that will distinguish humans in a positive light from the other animals of the planet. What is breathtaking is that it can happen as naturally as the sunrise in the presence of sentient sex replacing deceit, ruthlessness, and self-absorption which are the accepted, and often celebrated, order of the day.

If one looks at today, as a historian would, one would have to view the current sentiment as disappointed. All attempts to rise above have been abandoned. The continuous crushing of the identity represented by the aspirations of the human spirit has caused a lethargy that is difficult to overcome.

The insidious, inaccurate lesson is drilled into our heads, once again. Abandon all hope. Mankind is a mess and there is nothing that can be done about it. We will continue to live in squalor and disruption. New generations occasionally continue to fight the flood, but the flood continues. The cycles will continue as long as the root cause remains.

It truly is a matter of Yin and Yang, the serene female spirit and the deluded, disgruntled male spirit. The cycles and the struggle end with sentient sex.

This is where the wisdom of our instincts comes into play with the cultivation of the desire for honourable behaviour that was evident in the codes of conduct of monarchies, even though they were seldom followed. The same could be said of the Flower Power movement.

In both cases, our sentient instincts came to the fore for a little while only to be crushed under the boot heel of the edicts produced by the ongoing bane of non-sentient sex. We are more than animals. We are just deluded. The delusions take such a formidable form, convincing everyone in their despair that they are nothing more than brutish animals.

Everyone, in their delusions and despair, is willing to stand up and say that nothing is sacrosanct. Make no mistake, mankind, sentience, sentient sex, and sentient love are sacrosanct.

We will shed our delusions and despair, finally. We will recognize that we can be more than a grubbing animal willing to take advantage of everyone and everything because nothing matters. Self-respect will finally takes its place as a principal guide for our behaviours. Unburdened by the scourge of non-sentient sex, unleashed from the urge to self-destruction, these higher quality behaviours will have no need to be coerced into existence in men.

The technical and scientific accomplishments of the human race are breath-taking. Our human accomplishments in the realm of emotional stability and self-worth can now reach the same breath-taking pinnacle of success and slowly unravel the many millennia of misdirection. The attempts to promote the aspiring human qualities of three thousand years ago, a few hundred years ago, as well as the attempts of a half century ago to break through the sexual barrier and become sentient, will finally come to fruition. We can finally break the shackles that have bound us to brutish behaviour and outlook.

We can reach to the sky for our lofty goals. In facing our own self-image without regret, all things change. Looking in the mirror and respecting what we see with no necessity to deceive ourselves as to the person looking back at us, we will no longer need to cringe and turn away.

We can embrace the goal of overcoming the scourge and remedying it. We can banish it from existence. If there are a few left that cannot attain the highest goal of loving sex, through lack of a partner or lack of ability, they will not be a disruptive force to completely upset the stability of the human race. With the scourge gone, we will be able to definitively understand what it means to be human. We will no longer need to cower in the shadows from the perception of ourselves as a cursed life-form.

We are sexual beings *and* we are sentient. Sex can and should be a positive, central part of our lives, rather than a distorted, hidden, deformed sad by-product. Once we overcome our inability to share sexual pleasure honestly, openly, and satisfactorily and remove the distorting rut that mankind has endured, we can achieve true greatness as the human race.

The nail must be thoroughly and irrevocably driven home.

The removal of this impediment, our disabling nemesis, will drastically alter the character of humanity. It will allow the human race to move forward, finally, with confidence and without the baggage. It does not mean we won't make mistakes but the mistakes will be honest ones. We will be able to act like a human because we will finally be more than a deranged animal. It, of course, won't make humanity perfect but we don't need perfection, we just need an undistorted view of ourselves and our place in *this* universe, not the next, and finally become fully sentient. The rest will take care of itself.

It is completely true, especially, for a sentient race that perception *is* reality. Sentience must live with its perceptions. If the perceptions are flawed the sentience *and* reality are also. Deranged behaviour is to be expected. Sapience is not even a dream. It will only change when we remove the keylog.

This necessary step is not even a big step in some ways. It is what could have happened millennia ago. We have been ready for this step for that long. It doesn't take technology, surgery, or pharmaceuticals to solve the man's issue. In fact, they can't. Just a little wit and a little will is all that is now needed. Enough wit to get through the chapter on Techniques and Considerations and the will to see it through. The solution is so simple, its basic precepts can be passed on by word of mouth. We have endured the nonsense of non-sentience long enough. Any man who is a man will desperately want to make the change.

The wonder of women

What is startling and wondrous is that mankind has been seeking love for millennia. It is the most remarkable human concept that transcends the normal state of caring that is the standard for animals, even in the face of non-sentient sex. There is little doubt that the fairer sex, the feminine spirit, the more rational gender, not completely confused by the disturbances caused by personal failure regarding sex, was responsible for this continuous, slow, patient guidance in the direction of love. Only the absence of sentient sex has obstructed its attainment. Do you begin to see why the idea of women battling to join the deranged ranks of men seems so disturbing? From their under-appreciated, subjugated position, they kept the human race from completely losing its mind. Even that, though, is beginning to lose headway before the insane steam-roller of non-sentient sex. Women, in their desperation, are finally beginning to yield to the insanity. and join the ranks. We cannot let that happen. Those that keep their womanhood intact and perceive exactly where the fundamental problem lies, in the face of all of the distortion, are extraordinary and have my deepest admiration.

The nail (pun intended)

What can be more devastating to a man than to have his self-confidence and self-respect blown to bits just as he is reaching maturity?

Of course, the relationship between man and woman is much more than just sex and this book attempts to make that clear. This book is really about sentience, sapience, the potential for love, and the unnecessary irrational behaviour of mankind that can finally be improved. The male/female relationship has the potential to be transcendent.

That relationship is currently crippled to such an extent that it leaves the relationships and lives of most relegated to mundane existences with little meaning. This is all due to a single activity that has never evolved beyond the animal stage. The central ramification, the stone dropped in the water to make endless ripples, is that a man does not feel complete, his self-respect and confidence is ripped out of his grasp, and his woman feels unfulfilled. From that single disorder, the ripples are endless.

The inability to satisfy one's woman sexually has distorting effects on all aspects of culture and has expanded it implications since the beginning of sentience. Men's lack of confidence in themselves, masked by the ever-apparent compensation for an inferiority complex has been going on for so long that we take it for granted.

Sex and humanity

The emphasis that this book is placing on sex is due to the fact that the sexual act has been misconstrued and its distortions to everything concerning our existence have been reinforced because of an incongruity from our distant past. It is so very, very important to understand this fully, as well as overcome the ramifications due to the millennia long lack and the domino effect on our rationality.

That misconstruction is central to the ongoing chaos that envelops the human race and blocks the move to a fully rational view of life. The resolution is the channel by which humanity, finally, can begin to tap into the beneficial higher qualities of mankind without impediment.

The biggest challenge to defeating this mistake in our composition of life is the almost overwhelming force of the nonsense developed in many, many cultures and passed down to us from our ancestors that says we must turn away from any mention of sex, that sex is bad and should never, ever be contemplated. We must stare that nonsense in the face and recognize the ludicrousness of the edicts and the underlying disruption that it holds for our existence. We must not turn away. Finally, we must stare mankind's nature in the face and realize we can overcome all of the nonsense handed down from our past and tap our true potential.

The unacknowledged, unnecessary debilitation of the character of the human race is hampering the completion of the beneficent model of human existence. We can do so much better than we have, so far, as to leave one pondering just how excellent mankind could be and how disappointing our current conditions and direction are.

The real missing element to love (not so surprisingly, really, once we shed the blinders and taboos) is good sex. Our emotional aspects will not fail us if the physical aspects are not undermined.

To say that sex is central to human existence is certainly an understatement. We exist because of sex. It is the mainstay of existence and is something that is repeated throughout a lifetime on a regular basis, for better or for worse.

There is an additional component that comes from realizing that sex can be satisfying beyond anything else in existence. It should be the lubrication, rather than the sand, thrown into the gears of our existence. It is not only that non-sentient sex disturbs and disrupts everything. It is that loving sex can make a delight of our existence. Any man that thinks otherwise is still under the aberrant conditioning and taboos caused by our cowering fear of failure in this endeavor.

Sex is, of course, not the be-all and end-all of existence, it is only the beginning place - literally. In some ways, that is the point. The obsessions and perversions concerning sex are only prevalent because of our ineptness at what should be the most lovely experience we ever encounter.

Mankind has been handed down a distorted image of sex that disturbs the very fabric of our existence. Because the message that sex is bad and not to be contemplated is so pervasive, it infects both genders and leaves no escape. These skewed thoughts engendered towards sex are debilitating. It is perceived and often described as a nasty affair. It drains the life force from our very being. The corrupted form that it so often takes forces further distortions to our views on life. The mental models that result range from hating every moment of the act to enduring the act as an unwelcome necessity.

Without it being a lovely and loving experience, existence has limited redeeming grace. The profound ramifications are that, if sex becomes a salve to the psyche rather than a disturbance, then the rest of existence becomes respectable, appealing, and a privilege, enhanced by the wonder of the most enjoyable experience. Sex becomes a meaningful, fulfilling part of life. Everything in life has more meaning, focus, and acceptance without the distraction from our past.

"Making love" is not a spurious term. It is what begins to separate humans from animals. The obsessions and distortions surrounding sex are all the results of non-sentient sex, not sex itself and certainly not a sentient approach to sex.

The pornography, sex addiction, and all the other aberrant excuses for sex have the stamp of non-sentient sex all over them. They are a crudeness that a self-respecting human would never need to indulge in.

It is a reassuring confirmation of life when a sentient race finally can celebrate sex as the most amazing, significant, special part of existence. It is not something to obsess about, but a foundation for a life of reason rather than irrationality. It's not sex that is the problem. It is the misunderstood, inept, inhibited, suppressed, failed sexual expression that is the distraction from a meaningful life.

If a man can love a woman thoroughly and completely, to the satisfaction of both on the emotional and physical level, then he can have the confidence and surety in life that makes him human. If a couple can have the sustained feeling of comfort provided by an undistorted physical relationship then the foundations of life become rock rather than quicksand.

The open acceptance of loving sex is the mainstay of a sentient race that has embraced its sentience and existence. The dauntless determination to remove the nonsensical taboos and edits of our past by those most vested in them and embrace the truth would be a true blessing on the world. It would provide an honourable, self-respecting curtain to past mistakes that are best acknowledged as mistakes immediately.

Sexual adequacy is not a requirement of nature, but a requirement of self-image and sentience for which nature has provided most elegantly. We just need to recognize it and adopt it.

In tandem with it's adoption, dismantling of eons of misdirection and confusion-causing inhibitions and conditioning as quickly as possible will be essential. In most cases, the misdirection and inhibitions were institutionalized through figures of authority, decreeing nonsense down the ages. It is hoped that the current holders of these positions of authority will do their best to enhance the reparation rather than impede it. Again, it is the honourable, moral thing to do.

Freud hit the nail on the head, it's all about sex. It is the one and only raison d'être. Literally. Without sex, humanity wouldn't exist. Unfortunately, he did not drive the nail home. Sex is what can finally separate us from the common animals on this planet.

Sex is not the disturbance. Dysfunctional sex is. In its current state, sex continues to drag us back to the level of a disturbed animal. Freud's focus on repressed sexual desires was right but that was only a secondary effect. The real problems lies in the root cause of those repressed sexual desires. What is repressed? The recognition that sex is not all it should be. What causes the repression? The undeveloped sexual ability of the man and fear of failure to do so. Where he missed the mark, is that the most important fact is simply that sexual adequacy for men is essential and can eliminate a vast disturbance to our existence.

Another example of a man that had difficulty facing the facts because of the lies, inhibitions, and deceptions that interceded. He shouldn't be faulted for that. He was bold indeed, for even uttering the concepts that he did. He was, at least, searching in the right direction. He should be honoured for beginning to understand the significance of the sexual act and stating it plainly in the face of forces that impede the search. His lack of ability to pin down the root cause only highlights how deeply it has been buried beneath nonsense.

Sex is the very essence of the celebration of life. Due to this, in the absence of sentient sex, many of the portrayals of life currently depicted are of a painful existence that one must endure for no other reason than to get to the other side, death. As one pithy comment states it, "life sucks and then you die". All of the mantras that this life is miserable and needs only be endured until it's over are due to a misinterpretation of what happened long, long ago. The mistake is what has been endured for millennia. Men need to understand that sentience requires more from him than any other animal when it comes to sex.

The uncertainty that has surrounded this topic is disconcerting at best. Some profess that there is no solution at all. They suggest that, if you are burdened by this bane, too bad. It's not going to get better. Mankind has accepted defeat in this area without even an attempt.

This may be the only area in which mankind has not even made a concerted attempt to achieve its goals. The most important goal of our existence has been ignored. The gauntlet was thrown down without anyone noticing. The blinders were too complete for us to delve into the subject with any enthusiasm. What creeps into the thought processes of a man is that one's own satisfaction is what counts because the alternative of developing a sentient sexual ability seems hopeless. *That* is where the whole human system began to fail.

No man has ever wanted to admit that they are sexually inadequate because no hope of a remedy has been apparent. Much of humanity's struggle is due to the self-perceived emasculation of the individual male and the many varied, and sometimes, completely bizarre compensation techniques attempted. For the sake of the integrated self-image, it is easier to find some other irrational way to prove one's manliness. Let's develop that integrated self-image by finally learning how to make love.

Techniques and considerations

The art of loving

The art of loving is very closely tied to the art of living. The disruptions to the art of living that we have endured are due to our inability to construct that art of loving into something fulfilling. We can seek the art of living as something extraordinarily beautiful. The art of loving, in its most intimate form involving two people, begins with the the physical and that is what has been lacking throughout our history. It is so incredibly important the we have lost our way without it.

There is nothing in this universe that precludes beauty, just look around you. It is only our lack in the art of loving that limits humanity's potential for beauty. Our inability to completely appreciate the potential beauty of our existence is because we failed miserably at the physical component of love, sex. The emotional component suffers in the wake of that failure. The emotional component affects our perceptions. When the emotions are in turmoil, it is very difficult to appreciate the beauty of existence. Sentient love will enable the beauty of this existence to be appreciated by humanity. We will be able to live in a satisfying now rather than seeking it in some vaguely perceived future state.

The art of loving is essential to having a fulfilling existence for the individual and the human race. It can only flourish when the fine expression of the physical and emotional components of love between two people becomes commonplace.

The way for couples to attain this completion of the physical component of love is simply stated. Men don't twerk until the lady sings but the lady does. It should become a cliche. In other words, don't go deep until you are ready for completion which should be at the woman's discretion.

There are other techniques and considerations to be considered but, not twerking, alone, should allow a man to last as long as he desires. All of the important techniques and considerations are detailed in this chapter.

The men should save twerking for when it makes sense: at her climax or second or third or …. when the lady sings. The lady's movement, twerking if you will, just encourages the process by assuring her stimulation.

The coordinated movement of the two will help assure the woman's stimulation without over-stimulating the man. Depth of entry has nothing to do with this. The stimulation point of the woman is at the entry.

Love, of course, is much more than just sexual stimulation. The chapter on sentient love, as well as various sub-chapters, get into this further as it pertain to human life in general. Many of the aspects that pertain to the intimate relationship between a couple are discussed throughout this chapter.

The culmination of all of this is not just making physical love but of sentient love finally flourishing. Competency at the physical aspects of making love is just the necessary starting place where we have failed utterly up until this point in time.

Both men and women should read the section on 'Stimulating the woman'. Beyond twerking, it is the next most important aspect to understand. Some women are much more easily stimulated than others. The sexual stimulation of the woman goes far beyond the physical components, as well. This is critically important to understand. Just being loved, is an incredibly powerful stimulant for a woman. This may even prove to be the case for men once they no longer fear failure.

The lack of ability to sustain an erection just precludes any hope of adequately addressing the first, physical step towards arrival at sentient love, thus disabling the whole process. If a man is failing at the physical aspects of love, then the rest of the aspects of a loving relationship and the broader implications of sentient love can never develop. Once the loving relationship develops, then the emotional aspects can radiate outwards to enclose the rest of the human race. The human race's attempts at sentient love and a sentient, sapient existence have been stunted until now due to nothing more than the undeveloped physical competency at love.

The question to be asked and answered is what causes the ejaculation process of a man? There are four components to this physical process. These components are the erection, the stimulation of the glans (head), the buildup of sperm and other components of the semen since the last sexual release, and the movements performed during sex.

The erection itself does not cause ejaculation if no stimulus or movement is involved, unless the buildup of the components of the semen are just too excessive. In that case, nothing is going to stop the ejaculation. Over-stimulation of the glans can cause ejaculation but that is not encountered during normal sex. This over-stimulation is usually encountered during some other form of stimulation, such as self-stimulation. Over-stimulation is something to be avoided at all costs because it may become a learned response and also over-sensitize the glans. That leaves only the movement.

Always remember, the real point is that currently the woman often does not share in the orgasmic pleasure of sex due to a lot of nonsense from our past. While the man's orgasm is almost assured, the woman's orgasm requires a sentient male, that is a human rather than an animal, to find some way for her to reach orgasm. It is the delight of a man's life to have his woman reach this state as regularly as the man.

Stimulating the woman

The glans, or nub, of the clitoris is the most sensitive erogenous zone for the woman. It is the equivalent of the head (glans) of the penis for the man. It is the primary source of sexual pleasure for the woman. It is the primary source of a woman's orgasm.

The nub that develops just above the vagina opening, at the top of the lips, during sexual stimulation of a woman is the exposed portion of the clitoris. The clitoris extends to both sides, like two wishbones (the bulbs and the corpus cavernosum) on each side of the vagina. These split from the shaft attached to the nub to wraps around the vagina. While the nub is the most sensitive area, all of the clitoris is involved in the orgasm.

Interestingly enough, the corpus cavernosum of the clitoris is erectile tissue. This extension of the clitoris to surround the vagina actually tightens the vagina when aroused. This makes it clear why penetrative sex is much more satisfying for a woman than just external stimulation. More of the stimulative tissue is involved. Still, the glans of the clitoris is essential to stimulate but extremely sensitive. It needs to be treated carefully during arousal.

The rule of thumb

Stimulation of the glans of the clitoris can be a challenge during sexual intercourse, due to the distance from the glans (nub or button) of the clitoris to the vagina opening which, in some cases, is rather far. This is just another reason why the man needs to be able to last for some time and, also, why deep thrusts may not help at all.

The distance from the tip of the thumb to the first joint is a good indicator of how difficult it will be to stimulate the woman into orgasm. If the distance is less than the thumb's first joint, then sexual stimulation for the woman should be relatively easy. If it is further than the length of the first joint, the woman's stimulation may prove challenging indeed.

Considerations

Stimulation of the clitoris is almost certain to achieve the woman's climax. It is the main stimulation point for a woman. The thrusting of the woman's hips is very likely to help her body achieve climax. The movement as well as the timing will help assure that the clitoris' nub gets stimulated.

The clitoris' nub should be treated carefully. It has more nerve ending than even the man's glans in the head of his penis. It also has a shaft. If the nub seems to sensitive during foreplay, it can be stimulated by massaging the lips around the short shaft that connects to the nub rather than the nub directly. As she becomes aroused, slowly move closer to the nub without causing pain.

In the past, stimulation of the clitoris during intercourse has been a concern. The man's ability to sustain an erection by not twerking should eliminate this issue for most couples. If there are any difficulties, the next thing to try is positioning the man's hips farther forward, so that his chest is positioned higher towards the woman's shoulders, to attempt to position the shaft of the penis to massage closer to the clitoris may be the best alternative. The official name for this is the "coital alignment technique" (CAT). This will help almost all of the more difficult situations. Use of the fingertips on or around the clitoris during intercourse is almost certain to achieve the results desired. It shouldn't really matter whose fingertips are used, though there are good arguments for the woman doing the massaging of the clitoris. Another possibility is to achieve the first climax for the woman before coitus, during foreplay. As already mentioned, just be careful stimulating the clitoris. After the woman has achieved climax once, she should more easily achieve further climaxes. Just remember the clitoris is the key to the woman's orgasm. Penetrative or vaginal orgasm will stimulate more of the clitoris than any other method. While any orgasm for the woman is better than none at all, it would be worthwhile to continue to attempt to find a way to have her achieve climax during coitus.

It may very well be that this lack of knowledge of the importance and techniques to stimulate the clitoris rate right up there with men's twerking as the reason so many women never achieve orgasm, at least during intercourse.

If it is comfortable for the woman, a technique to consider, though an extreme challenge, is to have the head of the penis continually going in and out of the vaginal opening. This will cause almost a pulsing motion on the clitoris. The challenge is that it will be an extreme stimulation of the head of the penis. As long as no twerking is involved it should be fine. It may be worth a try if all other techniques fail.

Men don't twerk until the lady sings

The biggest mistake made in the past concerning suggestions to avoid ejaculation is that the goal was always to stop the end result of ejaculation rather than stopping the whole *process* of ejaculation dead in its tracks. In other words, the real goal is to never let the process of ejaculation even begin until you are ready for it to end. Once the process of ejaculation begins, it becomes overwhelmingly difficult to stop it from reaching ejaculation.

Twerking assures that you are causing the pumping action that begins the process of ejaculation, moving the ejaculate forward towards release, beginning the process of ejaculation. That is, the first stages of ejaculation that need to be avoided, have already begun. It is the deep thrusting that is the common cause of the ejaculation process beginning. Don't do it until the lady sings for your release.

The pumping action (flexing and relaxing) of the muscles surrounding the reproductive system, especially in the forward thrusted position (twerking), should be avoided. Keeping these muscles from flexing and relaxing too much in any position is advisable. The twerking movement, though, will certainly begin and end the ejaculation process.

It is worthwhile to describe the concept of twerking and how it pertains to coitus in a little more detail, since it is so essential to the idea of loving sex.

Let's start with a clear definition of what is meant, in this book, by twerking. For the man, it is the forward thrust of the hips and the pubic region , essentially pushing the penis as far forward from the hips and pelvic area as possible, attempting to go as deep into the vagina as possible. The deep thrusting does not help stimulate the woman even though that seems to be the normally accepted belief. It is satisfying and a good idea once the couple is ready for completion but, not before.

During sexual intercourse the deep thrust acts as a squeezing/loosening of sexual glands and ducts that contain the components of the semen; thus starting the process of ejaculation. It effectively squeezes the components of the semen out of their depositories.

It is the flexing of the buttocks to thrust the member as far forward as possible that will certainly cause the ejaculation to begin and end. Don't do it until the lady sings! It is expected that the metaphor of singing is clear.

If you think of the normal orientation of your pubic bone and anus to your hips, such as when you are standing, consider this the neutral position. Any movement forward of this position will start the process of ejaculation. Finding that point in the thrusting movement at which ejaculation begins is a learning process. Twerking seems as good a name for it as any.

In the case of the woman, it is the hip position and movements that assures clitoris' stimulation which may or may not include forward thrusts. The stimulation of the clitoris is achieved by the stroking of the shaft of the penis. The forward thrusting, the actual twerking may have a benefit in stimulating the woman, as well, just as it does for the man but this is not certain. In the lady's case, the desire is, of course, to stimulate as much as possible.

For the man, if the movement starts from the neutral position and moves back, and then, forward without thrusting beyond the neutral position, there should be no progress towards ejaculation as long as the muscles are healthy and under control. The semen will not begin its buildup and begin movement towards its final destination (i.e. ejaculation). The deeper (more forward) the thrust, the more you are stimulating the glands that hold the semen.

Once you begin to use this method, how far and how fast one can move forward without starting the process of ejaculation will become clear. It may take a little time to find that point but it is easily understood after a few attempts. As you become more proficient, the speed of thrusting may be able to increase. Practice is a good thing, right?

Keep in mind that the deep thrusts have nothing to do with stimulating the woman towards orgasm. The key to stimulating the woman to climax is the clitoris. By avoiding the deep thrust, it is much easier to position oneself to stimulate the clitoris. That positioning will also reduce the stimulation of the top of man's glans, the most sensitive area. It may be a pleasing thing to do for both at the completion of the sexual act but, even then, it is not a requirement.

Learning this may not be quite as easy as it sounds. The natural tendency is to thrust deeply, thus the reason for men's problems in this area.

Always be careful and start slow. Don't ever, ever be in a hurry. You do not want those muscles flexing and relaxing in a spasmodic manner, even when not twerking. It's just that the position of twerking is the most overwhelming reason for the glands to secrete. Enough flexing and relaxing of those muscles, in any position, may also cause too much massaging of the glands.

It may very well be that there is a physiological component of twerking that assures the squeezing of the glands and the flexing of the inguinal canal with little regard as to whether the muscles flex and relax. The twerking position seems, as nature intended for the lower animals, to assure that the process of ejaculation begins while deeply embedded within the woman.

Never fear, your member will still go in far enough to stimulate without twerking. As a wise philosopher once said, "It's only the first two inches that count, anyways." The clitoris is near the opening above the upper edge of the vagina. Depth of entry is not as important as orientation to the clitoris for stimulating the lady. If you position yourself correctly, since you can disregard the need for the deep thrust, the woman's clitoris should be within easy reach of the shaft of your penis. The deep thrusting is a legacy of non-sentient sex unless it is only being done for the intended conclusion of the act of sex. An interesting side note is that the positioning to stimulate the clitoris will also minimize the stimulation of the most sensitive area on the top of your glans (head).

Unless the man's load of semen has been building up for a long time, just getting an erection does not cause ejaculation. The idea that mental stimulation alone is enough to cause ejaculation only makes sense if you are either overfull of semen or you have over-sensitized the head of the penis. It is, of course, possible that a man, or a woman for that matter, can achieve orgasm just through mental stimulation alone but, in the man's case, that is certainly not the goal being discussed in this book. Orgasm through mental stimulation will not happen haphazardly. It is not something that will happen without considerable effort. We are trying to achieve the opposite and avoid orgasm until it is desired. So, it is not really a case to be considered or a concern.

The concept of men not twerking is all about eliminating the squeezing and relaxing action on the glands and inguinal canal that cause the ejaculation to begin. The further forward you thrust, the more you are squeezing those glands, and then, relaxing them on the return, forcing the emission from the glands that contain the components of the semen and moving it forward is the first step in process of ejaculation. In the case of the inguinal canals, it seems more similar to the squirting action of milking caused by the flexing of the lower abdominal muscles.

The forward thrusting and the flexing and relaxing of the perineum muscles in the pelvic cavity forces the emission from the glands. The perineum muscles are the muscles surrounding the penis, from the coccyx (butt bone) to the pelvic bone above the penis. These muscles are also used to control bodily waste. They are attached, on both ends, to a structure of bones that have little movement relative to each other. The thrusting and the flexing and relaxing act as a pumping action on the glands (seminal vesicles, the prostate and bulbourethral glands) that carry the fluids forcing the fluid out. The sperm is transmitted through the spermatic cords contained within the inguinal canals. The twerking movement of the lower abdominal muscles (along which the inguinal canals run), encourages the sperm to move forward almost like a milking action as those abdominal muscles surround the inguinal canal.

Eliminating the twerking movement of these muscles will stop the ejaculatory process from ever beginning. The far forward thrust, that is the twerking, is the position in which the components of the semen most effectively begin their journey and the ejaculation process. Up until somewhere near the neutral position, the movement itself doesn't stimulate the fluids into movement. It is still advisable to minimize the flexing and relaxing of those muscles in any position. Flexed or relaxed doesn't make much difference. Only the combination of flexing and relaxing is to be avoided. Keeping those muscles tight (flexed) seems to be the most natural but that may be up for discussion. It just seems more difficult to keep them relaxed. A semi-relaxed state might be best but harder to maintain. This is another good reason to perform the exercises suggested below.

If one is extremely careful in the movement (i.e. slow and steady), it is possible that further forward movement may still not cause the beginnings of ejaculation, but it may also just be completely impossible. The musculoskeletal structure in that area surrounding the penis may just be such that the pumping action is a certainty when one twerks.

As you begin exercising these muscles, you will note how difficult it is to keep the muscles from flexing and relaxing as you thrust further forward. Nature's primary concern is assuring ejaculation can occur, thus assuring impregnation and the continued proliferation of a species. It is also best, from nature's point of view, to have the ejaculation occur when the penis is as deep as possible within the woman's body for the purpose of making the sperm's trip to the egg as short as possible. You will also notice that the actual ejection of semen occurs during the forward thrust.

Alternatives

There is one other alternative that is worth attempting if it doesn't feel too awkward and works very well in some positions, such as standing up. Don't move your pelvis at all. Make the motion with the rest of your body. Move your whole frame forwards and backwards while holding the hip and thigh position steady somewhere behind neutral position. Basically, swivel at your ankles or knees (depending on the position you are in) and your upper waist. Everything else should remain in a fixed position. Go slow and try not to flex those muscles.

The one possible reason for attempting the deep thrust is to stimulate the clitoris if it is difficult to reach with any other method. It is possible to stimulate it with base of the penis (effectively, the pelvic bone against the clitoris) during the deep thrust. It will be an extreme challenge for the man to avoid ejaculation, though in this case. The man will still need to move slow. Attempt to stay in a relatively deep position while massaging through lateral movement and keep any thrusting as small and infrequent as possible.

For the vast majority of couples, just shallow thrusts and slow and steady movements should allow the man to last as long as he likes.

Going slow

Going slow is the second most important recommendation. If you are too enthusiastic in your efforts, you will lose control of those muscles and begin the process of ejaculation by inadvertently twerking and/or flexing and relaxing these muscles.

The point of going slow is to keep control of those muscles and avoid sharp thrusting that stimulates the sexual glands and inguinal canal towards ejaculation. Fast movement can be considered a form of twerking as the sharp sudden thrusts may also move you forward of the neutral position or cause the neutral position to move further back.

The muscles

It is a good idea to exercise the muscles involved in the sexual process, as it is with all muscles. It is wise to keep them supple and toned for a number of reasons that go far beyond ejaculation control. They also control the elimination of bodily waste. As an example, with these muscles supple and toned, you should never need to wear diapers as you age.

The muscles involved in sexual release do not get exercise in the normal course of events in a person's life. Also, these muscles are different from any muscles that you normally exercise in that they are not involved in bodily movement and bodily movement does not assure exercise.

It is a different effort to exercise these muscles. The only time the muscles are worked is for a few moments during sex and the elimination of bodily wastes. That is not really exercise. The muscles will lose all tone and may even become atrophied.

The muscles in the perineum, as well as the external abdominal oblique muscles (just think of them as your lower abdominal muscles, though you can find more detail, if you desire, online), and the upper thigh muscles should be exercised. In other words, all of the muscles surrounding the base of the penis. That is not nearly as easy as it sounds.

It is important to have these muscles strong, supple and coordinated. The spasming action of these muscles can also be minimized, though not not eliminated, through exercise. Once again, *delaying* the spasming is not the point. That will only delay the inevitable, not stop it in its tracks.

These muscles of the perineum are different from most muscles in the body. Most muscles in the body contract or relax in order to move the skeletal structure in some way. The thigh muscles, for example, can be used to raise and lower the leg or flex the knee. The "sex muscles", all of the muscles in the pelvic diaphragm, *have no involvement in movement*. No bodily movement will assure the exercise of these muscles. Their purpose is entirely different. This is what makes them so different and challenging to exercise. It takes only concentration. Their strengthening may also make it easier to regain an erection.

It is best to start the exercises when you are young though it may seem superfluous. It is better to keep them supple and toned rather than attempt to regain that suppleness and tone at a later date.

Exercise

As with any exercise, be extremely careful, especially when you begin. Weak muscles are easily damaged. Strong muscles not as much, but still, be careful. If the muscles are not developed as a whole set, strains can develop. If you sense a strain, stop, assess the situation and avoid repeating that strain, even if you have to take a few days off.

The best that can be expected from most sexercises, since these exercises concentrate on movement, is that they exercise the muscles close to the pelvic diaphragm (a good thing) and stimulate the pelvic diaphragm muscles only a little, unless the concentration is brought to bear on exercising them specifically. The body movement, alone, will not do much for these muscles. Unless one is aware that it takes a conscious effort to exercise them, while realizing that no movement is necessary or particularly helpful, there is minimum value. You could perform the physical movements of sexercises all day long without ever exercising the perineum. The sexercises are certainly viable exercise if the concentration on the perineum muscles is recognized and performed.

If you really want to exercise those muscles, concentrate on flexing and relaxing them. You just contract them and relax them. That may sound easy but it is not. It is a whole complex of muscles and will take a while to get them all exercising together (another good reason to start while you are young - the coordination is much easier to develop while you are young).

All muscles need exercise. It is just that these require a little more thinking than muscles that are exercised by movement. In the daily routine, these pelvic floor muscles are seldom used at all. When the voluntary members of these muscle groups are used, it is either for a few seconds while you are eliminating waste or they are spasming at the end of sexual activity. Strengthening these muscles and learning to control them will make the muscles more supple, responsive and toned and avoid becoming atrophied. There are many benefits beyond sex.

At least to some extent, the inner, upper thigh muscles should be taken into account also for a similar reason to the pelvic floor (perineum) muscles. While these muscles do stimulate movement of the body, they are seldom used as such. They are seldom exercised in any routine activity. Try to find a normal movement that you perform regularly that works the inner, upper muscles of the thigh. There are none. One exercise is a rather unusual position. The legs extended to each side and flexing the torso to the side from the hips, very similar to a few Tai Chi movements or sexercise. Bending at the knees for this exercise can add another dimension.

The pelvic floor muscles (the muscles in the perineum) can be exercised just about anytime and anywhere. It essentially takes no time since it can be done in tandem with any other activity, though beware the faraway look in your eyes (just kidding ... sort of). It doesn't take movement, so you can do it while sitting or standing or laying down. It *does* take concentration. Exercising these muscles doesn't preclude movement, though, either.

All that is required to exercise these muscles is to flex the same muscles that you flex and relax during the elimination of bodily waste and concentrate on the fact that they *surround* the penis and your anus. Exercising these muscles while walking is also something to consider. Walking is good for you and exercising the pelvic floor muscles while walking is a challenge and trains the control of these muscles while performing some physical activity as is the case with sex. Try both tightening/relaxing repeatedly and just holding them tight for extended periods.

One set of exercises that works very, very well is performed while lying in bed and just takes a very few minutes. Lying down, undistracted, allows one to concentrate on the muscles involved in the exercise. This is very important, especially initially while you are becoming familiar with them and learning to exercise them in a coordinated manner.

For a count of up to sixty, flex and relax these muscles on each count. It is advisable to start with a lower count until the muscles begin to strengthen. Doing so with the knees bent would be one exercise. Another is with the legs out straight. Widening the gap between the knees, with either exercise, can help, also, at least in sensing the muscles to be exercised.

Also, for a count of sixty or more, hold the muscles tight. Same suggestions for the bent and straight legs. Same suggestion for starting with a lower count.

These four different exercises do not necessarily all need to be done at the same time or even on the same day. Doing different exercises in the morning and the evening may be appropriate. Spreading the four exercises out over two or four days may also be appropriate, especially as you first begin the exercises. Just figure out what works for you.

In addition, since the lower abdominal muscles are also important, raising the legs slightly, while performing the exercises described above, is very beneficial. If it is too tiring at first, let the legs lie loose while continuing the exercise.

Just to note that raising and lowering the legs (with or without the exercise of the perineum muscles), is an excellent exercise for the abdomen overall. It is much better than sit-ups from a structural standpoint.

As you become more familiar with these exercises, attempting to do the two exercises of holding them flexed (knees bent and knees straight) while moving the hips (not twerking!) is a good addition to become familiar with the movement and control. Twerking is okay in this case, but just don't make it an unbreakable habit. Make the twerking an occasional experience, if at all, just to note the differences.

As with any exercise, be extremely careful, especially when you begin. Weak muscles are easily damaged. Strong muscles not as much, but still, be careful. If the muscles are not developed as a whole set, strains can develop. If you sense a strain, stop, assess the situation and avoid repeating that strain, even if you have to take a few days off. Yes, I repeated this. It is that important to be careful.

There are many more exercises for these muscles that can be found on the web. A couple of the word searches would be 'Kegel muscles' or 'pelvic floor' exercises.

As mentioned, the external abdominal oblique muscles are also important and a good reason for raising the legs during exercises lying down. Raising the knees slightly during walking can also help work these these muscles. You may just want to think of them as the lower abdominal muscles that attach across the stomach to the pelvic bone on both sides. The abdominal muscles extend to surround the vas deferens tubes and spermatic cords that carry the sperm before it is mixed with the other components of the semen. The vas deferens tubes run right along the lower portion of the front of the pelvic bone where the pelvic bone meets the abdomen on both sides (there are very good images online). These muscles should also be exercised.

This is another example of a topsy- turvy situation. Women, who need it much less than men, have adopted the idea of sexercise and men, who really should be doing the exercises, have avoided it! Once again, the most important aspect of all of this is: 1) Men don't twerk until they are ready to ejaculate and 2) slow and steady will avoid over-stimulation. 3) Flex and relax all of these muscles as little as possible. 4) Exercise. 5) Ladies first!

An over-abundance of semen

Keep in mind that, in the situation where there is an over-abundance of the components of semen, there will be no stopping the flow. It, then, becomes like any other emission from your body, such as urine and feces. The pressure due to the build up will, sooner or later, override anything attempting to keep it in. Unless, maybe, you are a Tibetan monk. It also can become a distraction and an unaccountable source of anger.

Considering the whole point is to change the situation completely and for men to finally be able to satisfy their women regularly and consistently, hence having sex often throughout their lifetime, over-abundant semen should be a rare occurrence. Self-stimulation is always an alternative but only an alternative and be careful, if it is found to be necessary (see "The habits" below in this chapter). It should never become the goal. The goal should always to be to find a compatible woman that is interested, not coerced.

Triggers

It is worth emphasizing, one more time. Go slow! Note that what this whole chapter conveys is that you don't want to start the process of ejaculation. Once you trigger the beginning of the process of ejaculation, it is just a matter of time before it's all over. You can fight it, you can use the more rational of the techniques noted below to delay it but you have started the process. The end is in sight.

So, go slow, and be careful not to pass that threshold of forward movement that starts the whole process.   You may or may not want to experiment, as you become more comfortable and confident, with what works and what doesn't. That should be up to you and your Lady.

The trigger of having been too long without release is, of course, different. Just don't let it harm your confidence. The Lady should understand. Just make sure to make it up to her and often!

Other considerations

Make no mistake, it is still going to take some effort and care to last as long as you need to please your woman, but it is more than possible. You will also need to be physically fit, of course, to last.

One factor that must be kept in mind is enthusiasm (another way of emphasizing go slow). In the throes of your elation at doing it so well, do not lose focus. Do not let the expressed enthusiasm of your partner distract you either, unless she is telling you it is time to end the fun, it is up to you to keep things going.

Getting too enthusiastic is not going to allow that to happen.   Get as enthusiastic as you can get as long as you don't let the enthusiasm allow you to move forward beyond neutral position or lose control of these muscles.   If you find you have started the process, learn from it for the next round. Some of the techniques noted below may come in handy at this point, such as stopping any further stimulus until the feelings subside.

Keep the focus on the lady's satisfaction. That is, of course, easy to do once you gain the necessary confidence in your ability. Keep in mind that it is the forward thrusting of those muscles that is the most important culprit.   The woman's situation is a little easier. Twerk all you care. From the woman's point of view, the primary concentration may be on keeping the clitoris in contact with the shaft of the penis and cause a massaging motion that is pleasing so, coordinate the activity to assure this.

The habits

There are many *really* bad habits that can be picked up concerning sex, especially due to self-stimulation. That is, stimulation used to relieve the semen buildup in the absence of that best solution of a willing woman.

It can be easy to cause problems in the instance of self-stimulation if one isn't careful. Abuse of the penis, and especially, the glans (the head) can often occur in the desperate attempt to reach ejaculation. Both the abuse and the desire to "get it over with" are really bad habits in which to engage. The abuse is the worst considering the potential damage to both the glans and the psyche. It can very well make the glans oversensitive, then you may have a real problem. Take the time to learn from experience what causes ejaculation to start (twerking, repeated muscle flexing).

Don't yank or squeeze when self-stimulating. Sex is a gentle exercise and mistreating your member when simulating sex through self-stimulation can make it nearly impossible to gain control over one's stamina when it is so desperately desired.

Self-stimulation, itself, is a bad habit if it becomes a replacement for the pursuit of finding a compatible, willing woman with which to engage. Any belief that it is a replacement for discovering all there is to know about women is a mistake.

Self-stimulation can certainly be overdone. The less you resort to this less satisfying solution, the better, as long as the lack of release does not make you over-irritable or cause physical problems. Now that one can gain the confidence that they can be adept at satisfying a woman, there is no reason to avoid, or even be awkward, in the attempt of finding a compatible, willing woman.

The habit of self-stimulation should never replace efforts of getting to know women and exploring that most wonderful gender. They truly are wonderful, and, in the absence of the fear of not knowing what sex is about, you may find it much easier than all previous generations. Only engage in self-stimulation in a very restrained manner, when it is really necessary, but do not let the lack of relief drive you crazy.

In a situation in which a man can feel confident about his ability, with no missing pieces, the potential of meeting women should become much less of a trial than it has been in the past. You should be able to approach women confidently, knowing that there is nothing missing, nothing of which to be afraid. You also may be able to avoid all of the crude, insensitive behaviours that have been men's lot in life for all of history until this point.

Know what you are about

It is essential that you assure yourself that you are stimulating the nub of the clitoris during intercourse (and foreplay). Also, be careful and realize it is just as sensitive as your glans, maybe more so. Stimulate it in a way that she finds pleasurable is the best advice. If you are not sure, work with her to find out how to make it happen.

During coitus, stimulating the clitoris may best be served by coordinating movement or even just the enthusiasm with which she enjoys the act of sex. In the woman's case, the backward movement of the hips may help the clitoris come in contact with the shaft of the penis while the man is positioned with his hips high. The coordination of activity will help.

Keep in mind, "Ladies first!", and even more than that, the ultimate situation is when the lady is in full control of when *you* climax. That may be the ultimate perfection of sexual coupling in a sentient race, the ultimate definition of loving sex.

If all else fails, go down on her. Guaranteed to work as long as she is willing.

While sexual adequacy may seem dry and clinical, loving your woman is not. It is an art form in which you celebrate existence, your sharing, and your Lady. It is about loving sex, sharing intimate emotions that have, so far in our existence, become curtailed by the spectre of non-sentient sex and all of the ludicrous shame we have heaped on the subject. Sex is about life.

It is near certainty that any man who adopts these techniques will gain the ability to satisfy his woman during coitus. Now that the knowledge is available, the distinction for a man being human or a brute animal, resides in his willingness to make the effort.

Everything else

One last interesting point about not twerking. During the research, a few men were encountered that could not reach orgasm. It is expected that twerking, when the time is right, is their answer. It seems likely that those men, for whatever reason, just never thought about thrusting forward. Unlike the vast majority of men, they may just need to learn to twerk (at the appropriate time) rather than not twerk. Twerking (and not) should answer all of the conundrums concerning sexual problems for most of humanity. It is possible that there are some that will never find an answer due to some physical or mental complication. It seems unlikely, though, that this won't work for nearly any man.

An overview of the other techniques and considerations that may be worth reviewing is contained here. It is worth noting that men have come up with some interesting ways in which to prolong the sexual encounter. Many are dangerous and many make little sense at all.

Strenuous exercise before and talking (or otherwise distracting oneself) during sex are two suggested methods to sustain the activity. If that helps, it is a reasonable addition. But, distracting oneself from the effort can also distract you from not twerking or getting too enthusiastic until the lady says it is time.

The following outline summarizes the studies. Some of it may hold some value, at least, in giving perspective.

Summary of best known practices

A. Ladies first!
    1. It's obvious but worth repeating.
    2. Concentrate on pleasuring your Lady.
    3. It should be your utmost concern.
    4. It should be all the distraction you need.
B. Maybe the most important additional suggestion is to do aerobic exercise.
    1. This will improve your overall stamina.
    2. It may very well, also, improve your sexual stamina.
    3. Certainly will improve your ability to avoid exhaustion for extended period.
C. Practice breathing deeply and slowly, while matching it to the movement
    1. Do not allow your breath or movement to quicken until it is time.
D. Pause during sex
E. Possibly change positions, if necessary or desired.
    1. This may be especially desirable if it is going to last long.
F. Mental control
    1.Keep the focus away from your own release.
    2. Focus on giving, not receiving pleasure.
    3. "Ladies first"!
    4. Marshal the confidence that one can last.
        1. It takes complete commitment.
        2. The very natural desire is to give your partner the same, complete satisfaction that you encounter. Encourage this desire, don't suppress it.
        3. Do not let anxiety over-performance limit your ability. Confidence is an important element of mental control. Confidence can be built through practice and effort and by being completely convinced that it is possible. "I think I can" may be more powerful than you imagine. "I know I can" is the goal.
    5. It's really all about feeling in control of the release.

G. Practice stopping all activity when you feel the ejaculation beginning. Let everything get back to normal, and then, begin again. Do this until you can control the release for as long as you desire.

    1. This last one goes against the whole concept of not starting the ejaculation process and should only be used as a backup solution.

H. Cunnilingus, using your tongue

    1. The only real challenge here is making sure that your woman is accepting of the practice.

    2. It will work, of course. As long as lasting long enough continues to challenge.

    3. it can also be used as a form of foreplay or a way in which to keep the woman aroused between bouts, if you are also attempting D or G above. The same is true if, due to exhaustion, you need to take a break.

It is not that any of these above suggestions are being endorsed but none of them are dangerous and they might help and give a fairly complete guide to assuring that you satisfy your lady, no matter what. And, that, in the end, is what it is all about.

The art of sexual adequacy is believed to be, by some, dependent on physical and mental aspects of controlling a man's release. Certainly one terrible mental habit is anticipating release, and basically, concentrating on your own final outcome. Invariably, though that is matched with uncontrolled physical movement that assures the man's release. The mental control seems only necessary to provide the physical control of your actions. Concentrate on your woman's completion and satisfaction rather. Concentrate on her joy.

Frantic activity certainly means you are losing control both mentally and physically, you are concentrating on the final outcome of your own release with no regard for your woman's satisfaction. That only made sense when there was no hope for her satisfaction and mankind was under the influence of the horrible conditioning that said that women were less important. In a world where the woman's satisfaction is common, it will be difficult to find a woman that will tolerate the lack.

You'll probably read, "go slow!" about ten times, maybe more, in this chapter. It is that important. Do not let any 'practicing' teach habits that are difficult to break this.

The fact is that the change in the situation, from non-sentient to loving sex, is so radical that many unexpected aspects may emerge. The most important of these is the fact that, with loving sex, the woman should be in complete charge of the conclusion of the activity. From now on, it should be up to the woman to arouse the man beyond restraint and release - when the time is right for her, which would be an awfully nice change and a tremendous breakthrough.

The best, most beautiful experience will happen when the man brings the woman to levels of sexual satisfaction that allow her to feel complete, followed by the woman doing the same for the man. The man struggling to continue while the woman works to bring the man to climax should be a level of satisfaction for both that cannot be matched in any other way. Whips, chains, blue pills, acrobatics and all of the other nonsense that the millennia of non-sentient sex brought into existence can finally wane into non-existence as a poor, failed attempt at sex.

One final point on the development of loving sex. It must be remembered that lasting long enough to satisfy a woman is only the starting place. It finally opens the door to cherish the woman for her womanly qualities. Adoration is the next step that leads from loving sex to a life of sentient love and removes all of the barriers to a rational existence.

Loving a woman

It is expected that once men gain confidence in their ability to adequately complete the physical portion of love, all of the other aspects concerning love will quickly fall in place. Loving a woman will become as natural as it should be. Just as loving the human race will be come natural, as well.

Keep in mind that doing your best for your woman should be high art. It is much more than just the physical pleasure. The other aspects of loving a woman just enhance the physical pleasure for both of you. It starts with every moment you are with her and making her feel loved. The arousal of passion should start well before you even touch her. It should be in every moment that you are with her. That is also part of sentient love.

As you begin the actual effort to arouse her, delay the physical contact for a little while. Words, tone of voice (adoring will do), eyes, pure passion, playful interaction, and showing the love and adoration on an ongoing basis are all powerful aphrodisiacs. When you do finally touch her, a gentle touch and strokes all over her body are a fine idea. But, really, find out what works for her. Find the places and actions that drive her crazy and expect them to change. It is high art.

Wooing and romance should become the standard, once again. Making the woman, finally, become appreciated for her wonderful qualities is in order and long overdue. While the main point of this book is to explain the problem that mankind has faced through its long emergence into sentience and sapience and how to eliminate the scourge of non-sentient sex, it is worthwhile to describe, to some extent, that to which it really is all leading. That is, loving a woman and, then, expanding that love to encompass all of mankind. It is leading to the man becoming, finally, a loving creature.

Mankind has a long way to go to dismantle all of the damage, to its psyche as well as the surrounding human structure, developed over the millennia, and in tandem, begin building up a structure that is built on sound, undistorted thinking. This starts with loving a woman. There is a lot for mankind to learn as we go. There are a few essentials that make sense and they are worth noting.

Finding a woman

This may be one of the components of loving a woman that may go through the biggest change. As men put away their sexual ineptness and clear the fog that has been caused to develop concerning sex, women, and life in general the whole prospect may change radically. There is far too much confusion at this point to really say.

Finding a woman with whom to spend a celebratory lifetime may be as simple as finding a friend, once the conditioning and nonsense have been thrown out. Or, it may be the exact opposite. It may be that finding a woman that astonishes you in every way is essential and worth the effort and just as difficult as it is today. On this subject, about all that is worth saying is that it is not just about lust, it is not just something to check off on a list of todos, it is about the ultimate closeness you can ever know.

Has compatibility been impeded by the scourge of non-sentient sex? There is no doubt. Will it make finding a woman that is compatible much easier? There is little doubt. What is clear is that a great deal of the awkwardness between men and women is certainly due to the clumsy way in which we have approached sex.

For a love to really flourish, both need to be willing to put the love and desires of the other over their own requirements. That may be more natural than we currently think. It is a certainty that if *both* adore the other beyond all measure and are willing to do what it takes to learn about the other's interests, put the other's welfare before their own, then the loving relationship has the best chances of flourishing. Will this continue to be a necessity? Maybe not. What is unknown is how difficult finding someone to spend a lifetime with will be in a world of loving sex. This is addressed elsewhere in this book. If all of mankind becomes significantly more pleasant as should be expected, the game changes so radically as to leave the door open for radically changed expectations. A large part of compatibility may, then, be just a matter of being truly human. It is certainly clear that spending a lifetime with someone in a copacetic, rather than mundane, state will, at least, become a realistic expectation. It may be as natural as life itself.

Wooing a woman

Wooing is, of course, an important part of the process of the art of loving, though the interpretation of what wooing requires may change in the world of loving sex, the necessity should remain. The importance and effort of courtship will do nothing but increase as we progress into a sentient, sapient future, thought it may just become the natural desires of caring in a sentient manner. It may also transform radically from the perceived expectations of today. In the extreme, it could be as easy as just meeting a woman.

The man's confidence as a loving sexual being should make this activity something never before encountered. It is that men, in their confidence, can now get to cherishing, celebrating, and adoring the female gender without the ludicrous worrying about their manhood. Their manhood will have nothing to fear any longer. We can finally recognize just how the woman's loving nature has saved us from the brink of destruction that men have, in the past, been so determined to reach.

A real relationship is built on meeting and learning about people in general and the opposite sex in particular. That is the starting point, not just infatuation, as it has been in the past.

Lust is a poor guide. Especially when driven by a desperate desire to just find someone, anyone, that will accept you and tolerate the inadequate sex. With a complete self-image, a man can finally explore building relationships of caring that build a life of fulfillment.

A past belief that was surely true at the time was that people change. How much that is true of mates when there is no friction from unsatisfying sex remains to be seen but the expectation is that it is not true at all. Was non-sentient sex the primary reason that people in a relationship seemed to change radically and become unaccepting of each other over a lifetime? There is a lot of evidence to make one believe that this is true. There are enough instances of couples that have had some level of pleasing, satisfying sex for both that go relatively blissfully through life. They are easy to recognize. It is mostly seen in the serenity of the woman, the unfeigned confidence of the man.

It is going to become a brave new world. Until it is better defined, it is probably worth the effort to take the time to get to know the person that you think you desire as a mate for a lifetime before jumping into that lifetime commitment.

Keep in mind that you should no longer be seeking someone's approval. That's always been fool's gold and is another remnant of non-sentient sex. With the damaged self-confidence and assurance of sexual inadequacy and the disruption of the sexual situation, seeking an outside source of approval became common and could never work. If one is not approving of oneself, outside approval and acceptance won't help. You need your own approval which should be much less of a problem in the absence of inadequate sexual ability and self-respect or, in the woman's case, the uncertainty caused by unstable, distorted personalities of men.

You are no longer asking the other for approval or a blessing on who you are. You are no longer looking for someone that is willing to accept poor sex. You are asking if this person fits into your life like the most important missing jigsaw puzzle piece in your life completing that life just as the sex is finally allowing the completion each other.

That is the groundwork for wooing but what are the practices? That will depend very much on where you live, what your sub-culture defines. Conversation is certainly critical, of course, in any culture. It is the most fundamental step in finding someone with whom you share interest. In the world of sentient sex, the blindness of such efforts that has always existed should fade.

In most societies, there is some form of dancing and that should always be a good place to start activities. Ballroom dancing and many other forms are conducive to wooing and romance. Men, in some cultures shun many forms of dancing as 'unmanly'. This should fade away in the absence of all aberrant forms of manliness, masculinity.

Generally, you are trying to show the woman you care about her and see if she feels the same way. This will all be done in the context of the culture and sub-culture in which you live. Flowers, dancing, picnics are just a few possibilities, but it will all come down to what it is really all about, what pleases her. If what pleases her does not please you, then you have an answer.

It is all about learning about the woman that you think you desire and what she likes and what she doesn't like. Maybe the most challenging is wooing a woman long distance. That means, that everything is going to be almost entirely dependent on your words. A challenge indeed. It seems it could take lifetimes.

Wooing may be thought of as the stage where you are attempting to know the woman of interest, gain the woman's interest and explore the possibilities. It is also expected that all of the lying, misrepresentation and false hopes of the past will fall by the wayside. Romancing is the extension of wooing to continue to explore that most amazing woman over a lifetime, keep that interest, and loving feeling over a lifetime.

Wooing is just the starting point. Romance is the long term effort that lasts a lifetime in a valid relationship. Romance should be considered nothing more than a celebration of life with the person with whom you wish to share that life. It is as much about the couple than it is about each individual within the relationship. Both are a celebration of each other, or should be in a rational world in which loving sex erases all of the aberrations of courtship and loving.

Romance is, of course, also a critical part of wooing a woman. It is the long term aspect of wooing. If wooing is getting the woman to learn to love you, because you have shown her that you care about her more than any other could, then romance is the long-term passion and celebration of that relationship. It should be the most celebratory aspect of life.

Assuring that the romance lasts a lifetime is the challenge that was seldom accepted in the past and was even less often achieved for what are now becoming obvious reasons. It has nothing to do with the humdrum aspects of a lifetime or Venus and Mars. The destructive differences in the past between man and woman were based on the two inaccurate forms of love that developed in a race that was dominated by sentience and non-sentient love. The man craved sex and the woman was forced to crave security and the two cravings became consonant with the incapacitated description of love.

What does romancing entail? Making your loved one feel loved. In many parts of the world, the swing and sway of some forms of dancing (personal preference is ballroom) reflect the idea that the man takes the lead in caring and cherishing his lady. That cannot be beat. Some form of romantic dancing seems a good idea as a regular occurrence with a loving couple.

These are all thoughts that are perceived in the midst of an existence that is filled with non-sentient sex. How much it will change in the future remains to be seen. Who knows? It may very well become simplicity itself for two people to come together for a lifetime and celebrate every moment together. In this area, in particular, the unknowns created by really knowing how to love may create a completely new vista. When one can truly, fully open their heart, the dimensions of the transformation seem impossible to imagine.

The romance

Romance is really no more than extending the wooing for a lifetime in every way. It is a lifelong exploration of the one you love and what she desires, in every way, which makes it seem that men, not women, should have always been the ones that led the efforts of love. It continues to become more obvious why we have had so much trouble.

The central and definitive essence of love, the sentient form of caring, when it comes to that fullest form of the expression of love between two humans, is that it is expressed physically, as well as emotionally. It is something much more than just the sex and the normal caring. Romance is a very important component of this ultimate form of caring. It is just the passing touch because one wants to feel that person they love so much. It is the adoring gaze and so much more. It should become so natural that no lessons are required.

The best reference found, to date, on expressing love for another person, has been found in the "The Five Languages of Love" by Gary Chapman. It shows clearly how romance is a multi-faceted form of caring that is dependent on the needs and desires of the other. It may be a serious challenge to read for those men that are still bogged down in the current misperceptions of manliness. Please make the effort. It is worth your while.

Romance may best be described as sharing. Sharing a dance on the dance floor, sharing the chores at home, or sharing an effort, sharing time, sharing your innermost thoughts and desires, sharing your life. Maybe that effort is as simple as checking the finances or as enduring as writing a book or writing a poem for, or reading a poem to the one you love in an attempt to convey that love in as many forms as possible.

Learning to dance, really dance, like ballroom dancing has to be one of the best forms of romance, reflecting the physical essence of the relationship, that can endure for a lifetime. Dancing should no longer be such an embarrassment to a man now that he is no longer trying to determine how to be 'manly'. A man that is finally self-assured in the most important department should have no difficulty with the dance floor.

A massage (head massages, by the way, are just an incredible feeling) is an incredible experience and a fine way to show your love. Washing her hair, combing it out, helping with the little things, all of these are ways to keep the romance in the relationship. Learning to cook and treating her to her favorite meal in a nice atmosphere where you have set the table in a romantic way might be a nice treat.

Really, romancing is just learning what pleases her and doing it. If you really care for the woman, this should be child's play. You will learn everything you can about her because you care for her deeply. In the world of 'manliness', in some bizarre way, this is portrayed as shameful.

Basically, be creative, and most importantly, know her, know everything about her. Creativity should become a much more common staple of life in a world of loving sex and the prominence of self-confidence. The loving relationship between man and woman is a good place to start. Creativity is really just a celebration of existence. If nowhere else in your life, be creative in pleasing your woman and find out what pleases her. Once the seed of creativity is set, it is sure to grow in a confident individual.

Finding presents for her, whether on some special occasion or not is another expression of that love. It is the creativity in finding something that she will appreciate, not the expense. Expensive gifts are also likely to be a remnant of a world of non-sentient sex in which the woman is being bribed. Finding a present that she really wants, will almost certainly impress her, and more importantly, show her that you care, that you are thinking of her, that you are listening to her, and that you know her. What are her interests? Find a present to suit. This all can be done with ease, once the distractions of failure are removed.

As life together progresses, it is often extremely difficult to even find the time for romance. If you have children and all of the other normal aspects of a life together, finding any time for anything beyond the essentials may become a challenge, especially in our modern world. It's worthwhile to face and overcome that challenge. If you are lucky, you have rational grandparents that live nearby and you can rely on for some help and relief to give you time for romance.

In the current environment, it is a shame that many couples struggle when their children leave the home. It should be the opposite. The exploration should be able to start, once again, in earnest. The wear of twenty years in a destructive, disappointing sexual environment negates this possibility. Only the years of censure and recrimination that the failed sexual relationships cause are left.

You may notice that the focus in this subsection has been on men. As mentioned concerning some forms of dancing, the man takes the lead. It is time for that to happen in the affairs of the heart.

Loving for a lifetime

It really shouldn't be so difficult to find someone to love for a lifetime. The impediment of non-sentient sex certainly increased the difficulty, and maybe, caused a misperception that there are only a few that complement each other. Currently, people wear themselves down, through multiple relationships, until they surrender to the inevitable of a mundane, unsatisfactory relationship without the celebration of life. It is a compromise that should no longer be required.

A thoroughly accepted concept due to conditioning of non-sentient sex, at least in the U.S., is that people are just not compatible enough to spend a lifetime together. That people tire of each other. That should not be the case. It is a ridiculous proposition unless something is disturbing the reason of the individuals involved.

It was also quite a challenge to really understand things from the perspective of the opposite gender in the past. There was a vast difference in the sexual identity for each in a world in which non-sentient sex reigned. Now, that should quickly become something from the past for anyone reading this book.

In this new environment of loving sex, it is very likely that a relationship that was built on a solid foundation can last a lifetime. Only the parameters of the relationships in a world of sentient sex and love remain to be explored.

Relationships

Relationships may still be a challenge. But, they can be an honest one for the first time in history. All of the clouding of reality should begin to lift like a fog being burned through by the sun of a true sentient existence. It's about finding someone with whom you can sing. No games. Just honest interest or disinterest. The level of interest and mutual enjoyment are going to become the deciding argument. No more games. Are you interested or not? Is she?

Further considerations

Returning to the main topic of this chapter, the techniques and considerations for sexually pleasing a woman. There is no reason to believe that this chapter identifies every aspect that can be taken to achieve sexual competence and, by extension, sentient love. It just a foundation and an attempt to break down all of the taboos concerning the investigation. There may very well be more to learn about how a man can sustain an erection, without impediment or assistance of any kind, for as long as he likes.

This is the most fundamental change required for us to reach sentience. The pursuit of this most important goal should not end with this book. It is just that important. The Scenarios community on G+ attached to my profile page is open for any real improvements that are found, or, any disappointments encountered concerning the techniques or any suggestions that might improve them.

There is the possibility that more can be learned about this subject, as well as the full meaning of sentient love. This book is not so much a template as a starting place for the evolution of the species into a sentient, sapient state.

This book goes a long ways towards improving men's capability to last as long as they desire **without pills or other means that do nothing for the man's innate ability, self-respect, and confidence**. We need to assure ourselves that there are no further improvements that can be made.

The blinders should, at least, finally be removed so we can scrutinize all aspects of this sexual dilemma with the same unrestrained enthusiasm and unfettered curiosity which we have brought to bear on every other aspect of our existence. More, in fact. It is that critical. The interest is certainly there. The effort, up to this point, has been massively impeded by non-sentient conditioning that has made us look away.

All men should keep the following in mind for the immediate future. This is not your problem alone. It is a problem on a grand scale involving some large portion of men. The brevity of erection is common. It may take some time to learn the techniques involved to the point where they work well. If you become impatient, use the alternative method of cunnilingus to satisfy your woman and just remember, *this is not just your problem.* Sexual brevity without some method to redress is extremely common.

Another item that should be eliminated for both sexes is circumcision. In the modern world, it makes no sense to continue and it may have ramifications concerning sexual pleasure. Having your sex organ mutilated at birth can't be a good thing. It certainly leaves mental scars and may over-sensitize the glans of the man. For either sex, it is mutilation and should not be tolerated. If you are young and living in the U.S., realize that they will often perform circumcision on your child without even asking. So, be proactive, if you are having a child. Let them know you have no desire to mutilate your child at birth.

A last consideration

There is one last thought that needs to be entertained. Since the estimate is that there are approximately 75% of the women that do not experience orgasm or, at least, do not experience orgasm often during sexual intercourse, there is the possibility that longer duration alone will still not be enough for some of those women. Even in this case, the removal of the root cause of our woe is assured. The man need no longer feel responsible for the lack of sexual pleasure of the woman during coitus. From here, it becomes the couples problem, not something from which to hide.

Since the man need no longer feel guilty, since the man no longer need to hide his shame, the couple, and all of humanity, together can look for a solution without the disturbing undercurrents.

The overwhelming evidence, so far, suggests this will not be the case. If the orientation of the clitoris is taken into account, as well as not twerking and going slow, there should be very few people left in the world that do not enjoy the full satisfaction of sexual coupling.

Sentient Love

The most significant improvement that we will accrue from finally gaining a fully undistorted sentience is the sentient form of caring. Let's call it sentient love. In the presence of impaired sex, love in its fullest form, is just not possible. They are completely incompatible. This is why women can generally comprehend love much better than men. Their sentience has not been assaulted by the bane of non-sentient sex on the same scale as it has been for men. Pity all of the poor men that have had to live through it.

Sentient love may be almost impossible to describe at this point it time. It is a form of caring that goes beyond all bounds that we have, so far, been able to achieve due to the obstruction of non-sentient sex. It is certainly much more than the blissful, loving of a couple. Maybe the best guess at its potential is the blissful loving of a sentient race for itself and existence, in general. In its fullest form, it may be as indescribable to race that has not yet experienced it as color to a blind person. It is like all of the dreams of a race that seeks magnificence.

That we have grasped this concept of love for millennia intuitively, is extremely heartening. Latin has a double digit number of terms to describe the attributes of love that far exceed the stunted connotations attached to the concept today. Even these, in retrospect, will probably fall short.

It is, in fact, staggering. Nature prepared us in two ways to get to a solution and we have been approaching the answer on both fronts, slowly stripping away the blinders. Recognition of the concept of love and the uncomfortableness of the demon riding the backs of most men. Both have driven us to become complete.

It has been an ongoing effort on both fronts to resolve this issue, with one effort moving us forward, making way for more progress in the other. The attempts in the mid-second millennia to achieve the qualities of honour, integrity, and self-respect may be considered a cerebral attempt to achieve sentient love, while the Flower Power movement of the last century can be considered an intuitive, if misguided, attempt to overturn the scourge of non-sentient sex. Each guiding us towards the path of undiminished sentience. It is truly astonishing and heartening how nature provided for us to reach this state. Both are leading to the same goal: Sentient Love.

The evident waning of the more embellished descriptions and definitions of love as the common description makes it seem that non-sentient sex is almost like a cancerous growth that that continues to eat away at mankind's existence. We are becoming much more aware of the scourge with every day and less aware of its alternative.

It is interesting to note just how powerful our desire for sentient love is. The most fundamental form of sentient love is between a man and a woman. Alternatives have been attempted in the absence of this most valid form. A substitute grew, in its stead, in the middle ages in our desperation to find sentient love, a love that fulfills a need within a sentient being. This was the love of a god. This was noted very well in the book, "Conditions of Love", by John Armstrong. This is a very thought-provoking book on the subject of love for those that wish to delve deeper into the concept.

The need for sentient love, though, can only be completely fulfilled in its most enveloping relationship of a man and a woman which includes all of the many aspects of love, including the physical. The loving touch, the intended coupling, the sharing and celebration of lives leads to a integrated view that can finally begin to embrace all of mankind in the larger aspects of sentient love and what it means to be human.

While sentient love starts with a couple, once it takes hold, it will it will radiate outward to encompass many relationships beyond the physical relationship between those two individuals. The valid, rational, physical love between two individuals is where it must not be disabled or malformed or it can never develop into its humanity-embracing full context. The keylog stops the outward flow dead in its tracks.

We can only scrabble for the dregs of sentient caring in the presence of the loss of self-esteem and the accompanying emotional upheaval accrued by non-sentient sex. The inability to embrace that love fully is limited in a person that is incomplete. It is destroyed in a person that fails at the attempt. Both sexes and the whole human race suffers pitifully in its absence.

Sentient love is a sentient, amplified, improved form of caring only encountered by a unfettered sentient race, just as sentient sex is a sentient, intelligent, improved form of sex. It is that the caring and sex that is apparent in animals can be enhanced in the presence of full sentience. Sentient love consists of a knowledge, understanding, and caring, due to our heightened awareness, that goes far beyond what any other animal on the planet is capable of conceiving or experiencing.

The ancient humans understood sentient love much better than we do today. This book will continue to use the term sentient love to distinguish it from the myriad misuses of the term love in the modern world that have little to do with the central concept of sentient love. The term sentient sex will be replaced with the term loving sex from this point forward. The terms making love and sentient love both will be used to describe all aspects of the process and engagement of the relationship between man and woman and the expansion into the rest of the human race, the verb and the noun form, respectively. The caring form of sex that should exist between any two physically involved individuals is loving sex that is enabled by both gaining significant pleasure from the activity.

Latin had, at least, twelve words to describe the various influences and effects of the true essence of love. Today, we've devolved into a single notion for men's version of love: sex; the women's version of love: security; along with a whole host of lesser meanings that refer to liking something a great deal. It is so much more than that. It is what *should* distinguish mankind from the rest of the animal kingdom. Without it, we are just an extremely destructive force that is something more than an animal but not quite human or humane yet. We become a parasite.

Bundled up in the concept of love, each being a fundamental outgrowth that is enabled by self-respect, are many critical, currently enfeebled attributes including self-worth, caring, compassion, empathy, generosity of spirit, honor, integrity, responsibility, self-respect, respect, dignity, courtesy, grace, joy, decency and the celebration of life in all of its aspects. None of these, even the rudimentary caring that is common in animals, can exist in the absence of self-respect that has been the lot in life for men up until now.

While the lower orders of animals are limited in scope of caring, they are not handicapped by loss of self-respect. Their world view is integrated and in alignment with their situation. This is what we lost with the emergence of our stunted sentience and what we will recover with the advent of sentient love and loving sex.

Only men struggle with this essential component of existence. The concepts of sentient love are all founded on feelings of self-worth which cannot be sustained without the feelings of self-respect.

We have continued to grasp for all of these concepts for a long time, due to the grace of the feminine gender, but it has kept getting further and further from our grasp. The undercurrent of love will be fully realized when the human race eliminates the major obstacle to its rational existence and finally becomes sentient.

Women attempted, over and over again, to nourish the concept of love in order to allow it to gain a foothold, and yet, to no avail. They could never fully grasp the nature of the problem (and certainly not its remedy) that haunted men and continued to disrupt sentient love's acceptance. The problem wasn't theirs. While they may have had a vague sketchy idea of what the problem was with which men dealt, they could never fully comprehend it nor suggest a solution.

The initial emergence of both the concept of sentient love and the disturbance of non-sentient sex coincided with the initial development of our sentience. Sentient awareness brought both into existence virtually simultaneously. All we need to do is resolve and eliminate the disturbance to finally allow the long-awaited goal of sentient love to flourish. The women comprehended love and the men endured the disturbance. Now, men can also begin to lose the distraction that makes it virtually impossible to accept the concept of sentient love. Once the majority of men learn that they need not be inadequate at sex, the change will begin.

Fundamentally, love cannot exist without loving sex. The whole structure of caring falls apart in the presence of a sexual landscape that is unfulfilling. Even the animalistic forms of caring are compromised. The basis of sentient love begins with the couple and radiates outward from there, just as the disturbances have in the past. The very initial steps into sentient love fail miserably in the face of sexual frustration. The adequate ability and completion of the physical pleasure for the majority of mankind are necessary prerequisites. The adequate ability, the confidence that one can, when given the opportunity, pleasure one's mate is the essential foundation.

Sentient love is a grand concept that only the truly sentient half of our race have been able to recognize and express. There is little doubt that the less affected, more stable half of humanity, women that is, are the ones that were able to grasp the concept so many millennia ago. That it has never come to fruition was due to the forced derangement of the other half of humanity. No fault should be meted out to men. They were in the unenviable, miserable embrace of a scourge that snuck up on the human race. It's time to let it go, along with all of its demented effects that are so dangerously close to causing havoc from which we cannot recover. You might just want to feel regret for those that had to live in an existence without sentient sex and love.

With the removal of the disturbance to our sentience, existence can finally be moderated and balanced by sentient love. The indication that we are achieving this will be the reemergence of a single concept of love for both genders: caring on a sentient level that can lead to sapience. It will begin with individual relationships and expand outward from there.

<u>Love</u>

Love. Ponder just how remarkable the concept of love is. Not the cheapened version that is used today but the true essence of the concept. The word has been around for more than two thousand years. It used to mean something very, very special and was defined to a much greater degree. It has since become a washed out concept of little importance in today's world. Truly as if we are devolving. This is due directly to the source of our unreason. The two are completely incompatible. The continued existence of non-sentient sex grates more and more on the desire for sentient love.

From where did this remarkable concept of love come? Why is the modern version of that concept so cheapened? This is a significant example of an instance in which we have attempted to attain a higher order of existence and, yet, failed utterly. Even the concept of love has been difficult for humanity to define eloquently. While the vague concept of love continues to drive us towards higher ideals, it can never be fully achieved or elucidated until we put away the source of our deranging behaviours. The two are completely contradictory models of existence. One reflects our animalistic origins while the other reflect the promise of a future sentience that we have yet to attain.

The essential conundrum

How does a person love another when he does not love himself. How does a person love himself when he knows he cannot love another thoroughly? The undeveloped physical ability of men is the obviously missing piece.

Inclusion

The feelings of isolation that many sense are due to our estrangement from others caused by the lack of completion of sentience inherent in the non-sentient sexual model. A person may not understand how others view them in the confusion caused by that incomplete, essential part of our nature and the false front that has often been adopted in its stead. That facade acts as a barrier to inclusion. One feels isolated by one's own lack of acceptance of one's own character and unwillingness to reveal oneself completely to others. It closes off many avenues of expression and causes isolation. In its incomplete form, our character rebels against revealing itself. It is a concealment, not unlike the fundamental deception that mankind has also endured.

The fulfillment of the individual's character will liberate its exposure to the outside world, advancing the sense of inclusion. We are isolated because we sense that things are not right and it is mostly a sense that things are not right with oneself.

The integrated self-image is essential to eliminating the feelings of isolation. This also augurs the proposition that mankind can become inclusive rather than isolated once sentient love begins to flourish. Humanity can begin a life of inclusion.

Self-love

It is always said that one has to love themselves before they can love another. That may sum up this book better than anything else. Self-love, in particular for men, has been virtually impossible.

Love is first about loving oneself. It is an old saw but more true than ever imagined. If one can't love oneself, there is no hope for that person to have any comprehension of loving someone else or even accepting love when given. A man who fails at sex cannot love himself. That describes a large subset of men which pollutes every aspect of our existence. With this impediment gone, mankind can begin to pick up the pieces and build a house that can withstand the vagaries of this universe.

Self-love, especially in the case of the man, will enable the change that must happen.

The expansion of love

It seems very likely that there is another aspect of life that we have gotten topsy-turvy. Rather than seeking the love of one person, it may be more consistent for a truly sentient, sapient being to begin the journey to the love of one by loving all of mankind when the expectation is that others will do the same. Inclusion rather than isolation, once again.

Loving all of mankind requires the confidence and self-assurance that is provided by the knowledge that one is sexually adequate (self-love enabled). This is something what women have always provided with ease. We *should* be able to love all but the conditions to do so were just not in place. When people can finally trust themselves to be honourable, they will also trust others to do the same. It won't happen overnight.

Particular love

Finding the love of a particular one with whom to spend a lifetime will still be essential and far more fulfilling than it ever has been before, but it is difficult to determine whether this will be more easily done in the future or not. It seems that, as more people becoming truly capable of sentient love, it will be easier to find a mate but there are certain qualities within a person that may reach far beyond the scope of just being capable of sentient love that may remain important.

Making love

The term 'making love', in this instance, is meant to describe the full panoply of love. A prominent emphasis is placed on the emotional aspects enabled by the beneficial completion of the physical aspects between two people. That is, the emotional stability being unimpeded by the delusions brought on by non-sentient sex. These emotional aspects of the individual should encompass the whole of the human race when it resides most prominently within the relationship expressed between two individuals. It is the unleashing of the force of the celebration of life.

The true measure of an individual is how deeply and thoroughly they can love in a sentient manner. This is why the emotional aspects require emphasis.

This ability has almost atrophied in men and, yet, it can begin to return in a single generation when the men learn the physical aspects of love. Then, men can finally hold their heads high, learn the emotional aspects of love, as well as what it really means to be manly without the subterfuge and nonsense, and the human race can move forward.

The road to the ability of making love in its broader senses, for men, may be difficult. Being able to redefine one's nature in a way that radically departs from the existing perception may initially be a brave, complicated endeavor. What components of a man's character are essential and what components are driven by the subterfuge of non-sentient sex? It seems like the role of protector of the family, for instance, still makes sense. Hopefully, the need to protect from the ravages of mankind lessens enormously but it seems possible that the role itself will remain in tact.

The obvious corollary is that men would take the lead role of protecting the human race from any outside forces of destruction but that may not be as true. The types of forces that mankind will need to battle, once we can obliterate the fighting of mankind against itself, will not be as much a battle that requires physical strength as it will require mental wit and determination. This is just as suited to a woman as it is a man. In fact, some of the experiences of womanhood requires a test of determination that a man never encounters.

The physical portion of making love is the most basic and, yet, the most essential part of making love. All also depends on its satisfactory completion, in a sentient sense. When the physical facets of making love fail, then all of the promise, all of the potential that is bound up in making love fail.

We have not even begun to see the potential for life in which humanity embraces making love. Making love is something that happens throughout a lifetime, not just something that you do in the throes of sex. It should be an integral part of our existence. It is something that should be coincident with every moment of your life. Expanding it outward from there into a celebration of existence rather than a denial is the essence. It should expand outward to encompass all of the human race and existence. The physical portion is just the beginning and, once it is restored to a sentient form, we can get started.

A lot of men may cringe at these thoughts of loving and being lovingly but that is due to the wrong connotations that have been attached to the terms love and lovingly. Love is not an effort for the weak. It is brave effort, especially in the face of existing forces. The most harsh connotations concerning manliness are the ones that are most at fault. The idea of needing to be harsh, brutal, a blunt instrument, small-minded and unemotional are just dead wrong. They are nothing more than an inferiority complex compensating for a lack that is embarrassing.

Relationships

The whole concept of relationships needs to be turned on its head. It is necessary that, with a completely revamped outlook due to the emotional stability provided by loving sex, that we come to realize that it is not only loving that special one. That, in actuality, it is embracing the concept that mankind, as a whole can and should be loved. Thus, finding the very, very special one with which to spend a lifetime becomes a simple task of discernment provided by the clear gaze of sentience.

This clear gaze will certainly take some time to develop. Trusting the human race, as a general rule, will take some time to develop as the individuals develop the worthiness of that trust.

A different world

It is possible for caring, trust, honesty, and inclusion to radiate outwards rather than violence, disturbance, deceit and suspicion. Today, there is an ingrained mistrust of others that is based to some degree on mistrust of oneself. It won't be overturned overnight. But, yes, we must change our course to that direction.

When one is confident in oneself undisturbed by one's own failings, in a world in which the same can be expected from others, the natural order is trust and caring. This will begin to gain a foothold on a much wider scale when deceit and subterfuge are not the expectation.

When caring is the norm within the household and people learn the fundamentals of caring in their daily lives, reinforced by positive experiences in the most fundamental activity, then it should become the basis for a caring existence that slowly begins to expand outwards. There is plenty of evidence that mankind is, at heart, a good, caring race in which a lot of that caring is just currently debilitated. Remove the keylog and the caring will quickly flow unimpeded. With the human race's natural proclivity for helping others in need, this will certainly be the outcome.

The Maturity of Mankind

The next step in the maturity of mankind is at hand. Non-sentient sex lies at the core of why our race has led such a distorted, disruptive, corrupted existence. It distorts everything. The way now lays open for humanity to mature into all of the potential that mankind represents. The imbalance that exists between material and emotional pursuits, between looking outward and inward, can finally be addressed. A balance in life can finally be attained.

Due to the advent of loving sex, the race can progress from being a petulant child unwilling to face its situation into a mature, emotionally stable state. We will begin to go through further stages of maturity as we shed the clutter of unreason accumulated over the millennia.

We can achieve some state of improvement rather quickly as loving sex becomes more common. Make no mistake, though, the full panorama of dysfunctional paradigms (think of them as habits of thought, a mental model) may take a long time to break. They have insinuated themselves in too many ways for all of them to be easily identified and overcome.

All of the confusion created by non-sentient sex may be difficult to finally overturn because it is just so pervasive and insidious. The first generation will still be conditioned into some bizarre beliefs and views concerning sex and life and will certainly struggle to rid themselves of every instance of these distorted habits of thought. The bulk of the immediate conditioning, though, should fall away rather quickly in the face of a stable mental state. Within a very few generations a great deal of change should be expected. The full extent of our disruption may take centuries to remove.

This next step in the maturity of mankind happens just as we are reaching for the stars, and also, acquiring awesome capabilities of destruction and creation. We, now, should be in a position to begin to choose wisely between the two. Probably the biggest remaining hurdle once all of the immediate detritus of non-sentient sex is removed is grappling with the ongoing, unavoidable, necessary, relentless, and accelerating nature of change. We deal with change now, but we are so distracted that we don't deal with it very well. Once our internal balance is restored, we will be able to make clear, concise headway in the right direction.

Unfettered reason

How much will a reasonable mindset affect the way we operate? This is the ultimate question as to how well we can progress once the removal of this major source of unreason is eliminated.

In the absence of a disturbing undercurrent, will the thoughts become crystal clear, will the irrational thoughts subside to such an extent that we naturally become sapient?   Every indication is that non-sentient sex is an overwhelming distraction that disrupts the whole thought process.   Clear, unobstructed reasoning should be attained. That still leaves the many situations in which there are no easy answers to be considered (economies come to mind).

Innate, uncorrupted honesty should surely reduce the urge to suggest nonsense with which our current existence is riddled. Much of this urge is driven by the underlying desire of a man to feel important and justify and compensate for a compromised self-image?   How much is driven by other factors?   Is the desire to provide an answer at whatever cost inherent?   It doesn't seem likely. Unraveling all of the past nonsense, though, may require us to make decisions and provide answers that are less than well thought out.

It seems a huge leap to think that unreasonable statements will disappear completely, especially as mankind grapples with serious issues from a past filled with nonsense.   In the past, when questions of importance arose, mankind's tendency has been to suggest and try anything and everything. How much of this was driven by unreason and how much driven by urgency?   How much of the urgency is due to our cluttered thinking?

Human existence is a complicated venture filled with a lot of information and misinformation. The final result may just be dependent on how much of the misinformation created is just a mechanism to cope with the complexity of existence and how much is due to the disruption.

Remember the definition of sapience: the ability to think and act using knowledge, experience, understanding, common sense, *and* insight. This seems a straightforward endeavor if the urge is removed to fabricate nonsense out of whole cloth to eliminate feelings of inferiority.

It may be that the biggest obstacle will be that we have put ourselves in untenable positions due to unreason. Finding our way through them may also be the biggest challenge.

Unfettered sentience will bring about unfettered reason, but we will still have obstacles in our path that will take considerable effort to overcome. The best expectation is that completely nonsensical approaches, desires, and squabbles between men, organizations, and nations that distract from the critical aspects of existence will subside.

At some point, all of the obstacles due by unreason will be overcome. That point on the horizon may see the biggest change to our approach to life.

All of this is a huge transformation for mankind and will not happen overnight.   Only the essentials will change immediately.   With confidence restored, the challenges will be welcome.   The horizon is beckoning. Saving ourselves

Why is it that we have always sought an outside force to save us from ourselves? It is an admittance that we were not functioning properly. The mistake was that it was believed to be inherent. That clearly does not follow at all.

We have overcome many of the obstacles and dangers that this universe represents. We should no longer be cowering in a corner when it comes to living in this universe. We need to learn to rely on ourselves and we can only do that if we are reliable and can work together as a single unit of life and light.

The evolution of sentience

In essence, mankind has not achieved full sentience due to the bewildering inability to bring sex to the level of sentient behaviour. The necessity of providing a satisfying sexual experience for both participants is exclusively men's issue and a serious burden for the man when it is not accomplished. Men will now be able to take a much more positive, less destructive view of their own existence which will lead to a much more reasonable human race, since their primary motivator is not that lack.

The infection of non-sentient behaviour was spread in a less virulent form to women, as well. Women, though, are not affected directly by the scourge and, due to that they are, by a long shot, much more rational than men. Most women retain some level of serenity and willingness to attempt peaceful coexistence. They are, though, affected by the disruption to their lives. Even then, there is a level of serenity that usually shines through. As the non-sentient effects diminish, their serenity should be expected to increase and shine through as a guide for the men who can finally really appreciate the fairer sex.

The magnificence of men

The magnificence of women has been repeatedly referenced throughout this book and there is no doubt. What becomes a very entertaining and heartening thought is that the same magnificence should be expected of men.

Unfettered by the disillusionment, bewilderment and crippling psychological burden of sexual inadequacy, there is every reason to believe that men should be just as magnificent in their existence. The two genders in that same state should be a powerful force towards our future.

Evolution, not revolution

Part of the historical perspective necessary to realize that revolution has always been a failure is brought to light by the fact that it never changes anything of significance. It is only the surface effects, once again, that are improved and even that is only slightly true and temporary. It is similar to the detective that laments that he puts criminals away only to be replaced by new criminals. Revolution is usually just a changing of the guard with little change in the circumstances.   It is still humans taking advantage of other humans.   The process of human interaction has never really changed for millennia.

Does this not surprise you? Does this really seem to be the natural order of things?   Doesn't the lack of significant, fundamental improvement in our situation seem like more of an aberration than a natural trait? The mind-numbing repetition of brute force, both in the revolution itself as well as the resultant situation, with no real, significant improvement in a highly intelligent race is not what one should expect.   The pursuit of nonsense without an intelligent goal, other than one's own grubbing needs, and only a momentary improvement(if you are lucky) in the situation does not seem natural at all in an evolved race.

What is really required is a sentient *evolution* of the human race itself, not a revolution in its technological, cultural, and societal systems that address only the surface issues. These only change incrementally and prove, over and over again, that as long as the race that builds them has corruption and deception in its heart, then the systems will suffer and man will always be willing to take advantage of any weaknesses or flaws in any system for his own advantage, as well as take advantage of his fellow man. This is not natural.

Mankind must change first. The evolution (not revolution) that is required is actually development of the more natural state of existence of a fully sentient race. What is needed is a liberation of the human race's emotional stability and elimination of the factors that destabilize. This is a very different evolution that is only possible for a race that is, in some measure, sentient and has the potential to be rational and caring.   Of course, as well, it is only a sentient race that requires this next step in evolution. It is just a righting of affairs. We gained sentience blinded to the fact that sentience itself required more in the area of sexual intercourse. It is an evolution that looks dispassionately at the past foibles of the human race, recognizes the disruption, eliminates it and moves on.

It is an evolution that is based on critical thinking but is spiritual and emotional in essence and guided by reason. It is the first attempt to purposely evolve into a race that can use its prodigious powers of intellect and perception to become much more balanced and attuned to reality that is not undermined by failure at an essential level. This universe is what we make of it.

There is a story of a monk sitting at a crossroads that is enlightening. A man, walking from one city to another, encounters the monk and asks him what the next town is like. The monk asks him to describe the last town he had visited. The man replied that it was horrible. The people were unkind and not helpful at all. The monk replied that the next town was much the same.

A second man encountered the same monk and asked the same question. The monk reiterated his question and the man replied that the last town was wonderful. The people had been extremely helpful, courteous, and kind. The monk replied that the next city was much the same.

This universe is what we make of it.

Renewal

Feminine and masculine characteristics have taken a vicious beating since the beginnings of the human race. The masculine gender has been brutalized by its own unacknowledged failure and the feminine gender has suffered subjugation, repression, and blame for a failure that was never theirs. The renewal of the human race will be echoed in the recognition that both have become admirable and celebrated.

What do you think? Time for a change?

The pantheon

Evolution

Genetic evolution is the only recognized form, such as that which brought mankind into existence. Some physical change, mutation, in a being that results in something different, like mankind's huge brain with respect to body size. What drives evolution? Instead of inspecting the seemingly haphazard or happenstance nature in which evolution progresses, let's look at it from a more holistic view. What is evolution driving towards? Some might say intelligence or complexity but it seems more definitive to say enhanced sensing and manipulation of the environment. If you look at the evolution of life on earth, it is an evolution towards a race that senses more and senses more fully. At this point, mankind is the pinnacle example on Earth.

A form of evolution has been progressing in mankind that has little to do with genetic evolution. It might well be termed conscious evolution or sentient evolution. It is the evolution of the senses and comprehension and the incorporation of the resultant understanding into our existence. In some cases, it obliterates past mistakes, misconceptions. In all cases, it forges our future, good or bad. It is recognizing what is really going on as we lift the fog surrounding existence. It is a new form of evolution and it is powerful indeed.

Our distant ancestors didn't have a clue. It makes one wonder why we revere them so. Altogether, our most distant ancestors were dumber than a bag of hammers.

We sense so very much more than our distant human ancestors in so many ways. Some of it has to do with our technology. We sense the distant stars and the smallest particles with a precision that our distant ancestors never could even imagine. We sense the workings of the universe and our planet far more thoroughly than any other life-form on earth. In among it all, we also sense that there is something missing. We sense almost nothing about humanity itself. Our strides in understanding humanity has been severely and vitally crippled. We have been duped on a single, critical issue and it has blinded us to so much.

The topic of sex has all but driven our race mad. We obsess about it, and yet also, suppress it. It is so central to our nature, and yet, we try to hide from it. It is one place that we have never sensed fully. Because of that, we have convinced ourselves that we are not a rational race, that we are cursed.

The curse is the lack of ability to celebrate sex as the most central component of our existence. Not obsess about it, not make more of it than it is (which is today's situation), but be glad that we have it and, now, can finally enjoy it in the mature manner that a fully developed, sentient, sapient race can. We do not use our senses to perceive mankind as clearly as we use them to study the most distant stars and galaxies.

It is easy to realize the immensity of the disturbance once it is recognized that non-sentient sex has been an issue ever since we achieved some level of sentient awareness, an immense time span. Something so fundamentally wrong with our most central existence that has been with us every step of the way from the beginning of our sentience will, of course, have far-reaching consequences. Something so intimate to our nature, when distorted, will also have completely nonsensical results, of course. It slowly whittles away at the sanguinity of our existence. That has been going on for millennia, if not tens of millennia.

It is certain that this single, critical issue is, at least, the most significant reason why we are so profoundly ignorant about ourselves compared to everything else in the universe around us. We have avoided inspecting the human condition thoroughly because we thought that what we would find would not be acceptable, that men might never attain the ability to make women sexually satisfied. That tore through every aspect of our existence. The false knowledge that there was something wrong and nothing could be done about it was at the core of our problems. That has changed.

This is, essentially, a new form of evolution. An evolution of our consciousness and our full awareness of ourselves by the removal of a situation that was blinding us. The most important evolution now has to do with mankind clearing the clutter and nonsense from its perceptions and recognizing reality. Then, we can move forward as a well-adjusted sentient species.

The progression

As mankind's sentience emerged, it began to sense everything surrounding it to a degree that had never previously been achieved by any creature on Earth. Along with sentience, eventually, came the ability to question and reason. These abilities, question and reason, driven by curiosity and a desire to know, could almost be defined as an extra sense.

The whole human race's emergence into sentience can be portrayed as an individual's progression through life. Just as with a child, critical thinking came to mankind long after experience and lots of muddled thinking had already become prominent with there was no reliable guiding hand. While mankind had gained the capabilities of sentience, it was sorely lacking in the necessary knowledge to wield it. About three thousand years ago, with the emergence of reason, the thus debilitated ability of critical thinking came into being.

It is not surprising that, in the desperate attempt to cope with this new sense and the realities of existence, mankind made some mistakes in its desperation for answers to existence that seemed required. It is the overturning of these mistakes that has been a long uphill battle. All of human life is built on inertia already established by previous generations, including the characteristics inherited from the animals that existed before us. It has taken millennia for mankind to begin to overcome the many mistakes and misinterpretations that early, undeveloped humans created to cope with these new, unique abilities. We have done admirably in most instances.

Our developments, though, have been in breakthroughs only concerning other subjects than ourselves, such as science and the material world. Everything concerning humanity remains obscure, vague. It is often considered that religion was holding us back. Topsy-turvy. In actual fact, it probably helped us retain some level of decency and decorum in the absence of sentient, loving sex, giving us a dictated form of morals to live by, in the absence of the besieged natural goodness.

Though religion was used, in many cases, to distort sex, it was not the source of the problem. It was just the tool to proliferate the nonsense. It was certainly an incomplete attempt at sentient love.

Non-sentient sex is the single most important lingering mistake for us to overturn. It retains within the human race all of the brute qualities of animals. Without those brute qualities, we will no longer need outside forces to tame us.

That nature has such a tremendous joker as non-sentient sex in the deck for any species that reached sentience gives one pause. A sentient race learning how to adjust its sexual relations in such a way as to prove that it is really worthy of the mantle of sentience is almost like a right of passage to achieve sapience and become more than just an animal. Once revealed, the brute qualities are denied and relegated to a very disturbing past. History will record a very distinct line.

A sentient animal that, if it doesn't overcome this disturbance, will most assuredly destroy itself. That animal never becomes completely sentient. The human race is required to shed the delusions of its childhood. Finally discovering that mankind can be sane rather than accepting insanity and a disturbed existence as a foregone conclusion.

Only mankind, a somewhat sentient race grasping desperately for sapience, could understand the injustice of non-sentient sex. The realization was unavoidable. The results required.

Inheritance

Mankind views itself in very uncomplimentary terms, all because of our early days of misunderstanding and confusion, before critical thinking could guide us. Even today, critical thinking is still muddled due to the exigencies of the past. The form that critical thinking often takes is a overreaction to all of our past delusions. *Everything* is denied unless there is concrete proof for its existence. That is no more rational than accepting anything and everything without question. The balance is still missing.

It is worthwhile to consider turning the whole thing on its head and begin again with the concept that mankind is, in essence, extremely good. Exceptionally good. It's seen in many children, unaffected by poor role models, and begins to become corrupted through distorted interaction and is completely overturned in the male post-pubescence. Examples of that goodness can be seen most every day in the common interactions between people.

It is often believed that this is forced by rules and fear. Topsy-turvy. The good comes first, its corruption comes next, and the rules and fear come last to contain the corruption. Even in the face of this terrible bane that has plagued mankind, the goodness struggles to gain a foothold.

People's natural state is to be good and attempt to be beneficent. We are mostly hampered by the existence of non-sentient sex. It is a huge leverage point to undo everything we could be. It may take more than just the removal of non-sentient sex to get to the full expression of that goodness but it is the most important place to start.

We inherited so much, beyond our genes, in the way in which we think and operate, from those distant, less able ancestors. Our earliest decisions, stories, and learnings from millennia ago still hold sway today. Many of those were nonsense.

The universe does not revolve around us, there is no such thing as ether, and we are not cursed. Stories such as these have been our inheritance. A lot of what we inherit from them in learnings and stories are conditioned into us while we are still young children before we begin to think critically. No balance is attained.

There are so many interesting aspects about this. For instance, another aspect of history if one looks at the whole tapestry from the beginning until now, is that it has been a constant attempt to break down the walls of non-sentient sex that is satisfying to no one.

The latest major attempt to incorporate the untapped potential of love into our inheritance was conducted by the Flower Power movement, Free Love. They sensed a lot about the problem and were so painfully close. We had finally progressed to understanding that love between two individuals and the sexual aspects involved were important and something was awry. A whole generation put its foot down. Once again, though, the shadowy figure of non-sentient sex slipped by. It was just misperceived as a vast need for love and an open mind concerning sex. They were so very close to the truth.

There were many of that generation that realized that there was something wrong. After enough of the non-sentience sex began to take its toll without an identified resolution that really worked, the wear began to show. Free Love or, more exactly, free sex was not enough. The people moved off into frustrated lives surrounded by a society that just accepts the status quo.

Do you also see the big, eons-long picture? Once sentience, the fuller awareness of existence, came onto the scene there was no way non-sentient sex would be enough. You can just about picture those cavemen getting more and more uncomfortable over the years and centuries, initially scratching their heads in perplexity, and then, just shouting it down to prove their manliness.

It should have been resolved about three thousand years ago, as reason emerged as a tool for sentient existence, but the blinders of paradigms were already in place.

The fumbled attempt during the era of monarchies, as mentioned earlier, to train it into mankind was maybe one of the most inept attempts in history.

As time progressed, the human race became more and more obsessed with sex and aberrant in nature. Not because of the old foolish view that sex was just obsessive but because *dysfunctional* sex is obsessive. The obsession was due to the continuously unfulfilling aspects of non-sentient sex for a sentient race.

It was a continuous blind hunger for something more: loving sex and its by-product, sentient love and a rational existence. In its absence, despair. The sub-conscious always grates over a lifetime at the indignity of the situation until, all too often, it all came crashing down.

It is the final piece of the puzzle that makes it all fit together. Sex can now be great. Nothing fancy required, it will be great just laying naked with your woman. What could be better than that?

Resolution

The removal of the crushing blow of non-sentient sex, should work in the same way as its emergence. The expectation is that the derangement should more rapidly dissipate since it is a purposeful, intended, sentient endeavor rather than the haphazard dismantling of our nature due to the discomfort, disruption, and ineptitude of an embarrassed race seeking to cover its inadequacy. Note that the inadequacy caused the ineptitude. As individual men learn to satisfy their women, many of the banes of our past caused directly by non-sentient sex should begin to subside rapidly.

Even for those that have sustained some past damage, due to a life of dealing with the scourge, the process of improvement can begin. The relief for those should be substantial. All of mankind can take a sigh of relief as it realizes that it is not inherently deranged or inadequate. This also should accelerate the process.

Mankind can be freed, at last, from the most prevalent enabler of the curse of deceit. At the individual level, self-esteem should also gather force rather quickly, especially amongst the young that have not been deceived for a lifetime. It is the many other less directly implicated forces that mankind has adopted due to non-sentient sex that may take awhile to subside.

This is not a problem that is addressed by legislation or any other contrived form of human force and control. It is addressed by the individual regaining or retaining their self-respect and integrity, improving his ability to resist any outside efforts to undermine it. This is the natural inclination.

The existing pressure of societal derangement will lessen. It will be easier for the individual to resist that loss of self-respect. It will build from the individual into a cultural evolution that will relieve a tremendous amount of stress on the human condition.

It is a grass roots, self-driven effort by the individual men. It is all but assured to happen. Who would not wish to be good at sex and be able to pleasure the one they love? This does not even consider the effects on self-confidence that, also, have been frayed and disrupted throughout the ages by this scourge.

Through the ages, unreason and deceit were the legacy handed down from father to son rather than how to achieve sexual adequacy. Sex was easy, just click it in. Does that sound very sentient to you?

The nice thing is that sentient sex is at almost the same level of simplicity. Just stick it in, go slow, and don't twerk until the lady sings! This could be essential, since it means that no man needs to spend years of effort to get a degree in sexual adequacy. The simplest human should be able to attain the state.

The avalanche

The analogy of a pebble causing an avalanche was one of many used to describe what happened to mankind due to the collision of sex and sentience. That minor inconsistency, that pebble, led to men becoming dissatisfied with their self-image and losing all self-respect. Rigorous rituals were developed that distracted from the reality of the situation and the avalanche started in earnest.
The analogy may also be used to consider what will happen when men finally learn to perform intercourse in a competent manner, feel good about themselves, and humanity can achieve the final emergence of reason.

Many of the most proximate effects in the realms of loss of self-respect, deceit, corruption, obsessions, and aberrancies should begin to fall away quickly.

As momentum increases effects more distant from the source will fall away in an accelerated manner as more and more men retain their self-respect and find their center. The wider ramifications are that mankind can begin intentionally seeking all of the other aberrancies and obsessions that no longer need to remain, as well.

The only assumption that is required for this proposition to happen is that mankind is essentially good. There is no reason, in the context of the discovery of the disturbance to mankind's existence and a close look at the background, to believe this is not true. The lack of goodness is not inherent. It is corrupted out of existence. All of the evidence supports the conclusion that mankind is essentially good, just disoriented and disturbed. The disruption that causes the disorientation has now been addressed.

The woman's situation

The worst ramifications of the past is that the guiltless women of the human race have been treated shabbily throughout the ages because of this stumbling block to sentience and sapience in nature's plan.

The most remarkable aspect is that women carried on, in their relatively quiet way, continuing to raise the banner of love and caring. And, they are still doing so today. It's just that they are finally getting fed up with the injustice of it all. We probably owe the continuing existence of humanity to the women of the race and this is not referring to their ability to bear children. This is referring to their ability to carry on and give heart to the race in the midst of the chaos caused by men.

How do we ever repay that debt?

Somewhat disturbing is that women seem like they will be the last to recognize the significance of this change. They have not lived through it and seem extremely skeptical of the change and the potential results. They may just have to see the results before they can truly, finally feel relief that the worst of men's disturbance is over.

The fact that many, many women realize men are disturbed has been reiterated many times, to the author directly, as well as in so much of the material that has been composed by women. They have also revealed, sometimes inadvertently, just how common sexual inadequacy really is. It may be that they just cannot grasp at the hope, much like in the past for men concerning sex adequacy, for fear of failure. It would be a heartbreaker.

Symbiote

So far, those who deem humanity to be a parasite on the planet and all of its inhabitant, including mankind itself, have had plenty of justification for that view. It is encouraging to now say that was a simplistic view only taking into account the current situation and not the fundamental factors involved. It was taking paradigms for facts. The distorted perception was reality. It was proclaiming that inertia alone rules and, therefore, mankind is essentially bad.

At the heart of the matter, we are really a symbiote that was disoriented and that turned much of our existence toxic. We deluded ourselves and took the pain out on our surroundings and everything we encountered, like a brute beast disturbed by some irritation that could not be relieved.

Once the non-sentient sex is eliminated, it seems a very real likelihood that we could progress quickly towards more of a symbiote model.

It is a bit annoying that biology textbooks have decided to redefine symbiosis to be a general term for different organisms living together no matter the relationship. The term now used for different species living together where both benefit is now called mutualism. It seems like an awkward mouthful (even worse is reciprocal altruism).

This book will use the dictionary definition of symbiosis, rather than the textbook definition to portray different species living together where both benefit, symbiote being a creature that lives in just such a relationship. To, be clear, symbiosis is interaction between two different organisms to the advantage of both, or a mutually beneficial relationship between different people or groups.

Game theory has proven that living (or operating) together in a mutually beneficial relationship is the optimum solution. This is just another reason to believe that our nature is good or symbiotic. We are distracted, not stupid. Living in a mutually beneficial relationship with all of our surroundings pretty well defines what it seems we should be naturally seek. The disruption of our existence becomes even clearer.

Mutually beneficial is the exception rather than the norm for humanity even amongst fellow human beings. It is not our current common human sentiment towards anything. Not the planet, not our fellow living creatures, and certainly and most horrifyingly, not even mankind itself. 'Mutually beneficial' does not describe the relationship between the poor and the wealthy; various governments and countries; religions; races; ethnic origins; lifestyles; or any other term for which mankind can define a divide. 'Mutually divisive' might describe the current situation best.

In terms of a future in which sentient love is the predominant characteristic, our interactions, driven by the reduction in tension within the individual, should transform into easier relationships in which mutual benefit can be pursued.   The obsessions that rage and drive mutual division should be mitigated by reduced anxiety at the individual level when the individual self-consciousness is soothed by feelings of self-esteem.

The force that stirs the humanity-wide uneasiness will have been removed. It should take about three generations for loving sex and sentient love to become the norm, as well as a clearly understood concept, and remove a large portion of the destructive tendencies that make us a parasite on existence. It may take much longer to remove the structural damage to society and culture itself.

There is reason to hope that it could happen a lot quicker as its seems mankind senses that something is not right at a very deep level and is only waiting for it to be enunciated clearly.

This is one of the reasons that the insights in this book are being so finely delineated. The more awareness of the potential of the prospect of coming change, the more we should be able to accelerate that same change in a beneficial way.   The more aware we are of the disruption, the more quickly we can address it.

Can conflagration, poverty, and hunger be eliminated in three generations? Who can say? These cannot, in any way, be tied directly to the disruption of non-sentient sex.   They can, though, be tied directly to the self-serving and disruptive characteristics that are the hallmark of non-sentient sex: the embracing of the animal spirit and the belief that we are nothing more than a brute and a parasite with little or no redeeming qualities. Despair at the highest order.   So, why try? Even many who may be considered good people in the current human condition spend little time over concerns about the less fortunate in this existence.

Mankind's ascendency and the unleashing of our natural goodness are the goal. Sentient love is the vehicle. Sentient sex is the driver.   The vague outline of the tremendous difference should become evident within a few generations, at least.

This is where the study of institutions and culture begin to weigh in and the answers can be considered tentative.   It seems likely that our ruthless, rapacious behaviour will wane without any radical changes to the institutions and cultural underpinnings.   What seems most likely is that the behaviours of the individuals will change leading to less ruthless, rapacious behaviour within those systems. Which, in turn, will provide a more symbiotic approach.

The cultural of our existence will most assuredly change, as the blinders fall away. Culture is based most directly on the behaviour of the individual and the shared sentiments towards existence. It may even be that we can begin to construct a culture consciously, rather than the haphazard, brute approach in which cultures have developed in the past.

The institutional structure is not so clear. Are the structures faulty, as well as the behaviours of the individuals? It seems likely that the structures will slowly progress towards something more amenable to a sentient race but it may or may not require drastic change. The most drastic change required is to the individual. Once the individual becomes stable and balanced, there is much that will need to be considered in depth.

The human race should be able to look around itself with a much less tainted view and assess the situation in the future. Again, three generations seems like an adequate number to have a significantly improved view of what will be entailed.

The guardians at the gate

Who are the guardians at the gates of human life? We are. We are the one that decide what human life consists of. So far, we've made a hash of it. It is now understandable but still true.

We have built tools to trim the hairs in the nose, extend the years of healthy existence (if not the actual length of life), correct vision, look deeply into space and the fundamental workings of matter. Now, it is time we take a close look at our fundamental characteristics and figure out how to make humanity something special. How do we, now, correct our course once this impediment to our existence has been removed?

On the very outskirts of the sketching that this book has attempted to convey, there are grand ideas of what we could accomplish, and more importantly, what characteristics can be expected to become common. It is hoped that others will take the time to continue to clarify. The interest, creativity, and will to do so should accelerate in the presence of self-confidence in ourselves.

What characteristics are just the remnants of a disturbed existence? The further one delves, the more apparent it becomes that they are many. Are there any left that need special attention and can be addressed in the current future state? Only time will tell.

Nature

If one inspects this existence we occupy closely, it conveys a desire for order. Existence itself or, nature if you will, is continually seeking a higher degree of order. The froth of existence, after the big bang, was essentially a cauldron of disorganization. As time progressed slightly, particles and atoms began to appear, a more organized form of existence. Then stars began to form. As the stars aged, they caused more complex atoms, leading to molecules, as well. Planets were formed. Next, life came into existence.

All of these are vectors in the direction of order. Life continues to become more complex seeking even higher levels of order. With humanity (or any other sentient race that may exist) the order becomes almost self-fulfilling. Not only are we composed and constructed of an orderly composition of materials but we also seek further order in our lives and our surroundings as a conscious effort. All of this could be considered nature in its rawest, most basic, elemental form: order is sought.

Sentience

As mentioned earlier, essentially, sentience is the awareness of surroundings, especially in context to oneself. Of course, the simplest creatures have some level of awareness. It just progresses with each evolution of life to a higher order.

A joker was built into the deck for our form of sentience in the form of sex. The balance is achieved in the magnificence of the perfect and elegant the solution to true loving sex. As if nature had prepared for it, which is rather remarkable.

Pure and simply, the conscious recognition of the awareness that the sexual status quo has not been complete for our sentient race, as well as the remedy for the source of that non-sentient characteristic, are a huge step towards balance. We inattentively wandered far from seeking order.

Somehow, due to the lack of a sentient mindset and the obstacles we placed in the way, we continued to convince ourselves that mankind is inherently irrational and needs to be regulated and told what to do and how to do it. The significance of these binders may still be under-appreciated. The elimination of those binders is the next step in our evolution.

Nature knows what it is doing. Now, we know what Nature is doing.

Sapience

Sapience is certainly something that we haven't even begun to approach. Reviewing the span of history, we have made attempts and failed utterly. The noble ideas of honor, integrity, and dignity were thrown out somewhere between the time of the downfall of monarchies as ruling institutions and the predominance of the industrial revolution.

There is an encouraging undercurrent, though, that is well described by the term 'love without borders", again, mostly promoted by the gender that still retains some level of reason. We continue to seek sapience and balance.

Sapience can now occur. As mentioned earlier, it seems very likely to be a natural occurrence when not impeded by a fundamental disruption to our existence and behaviour. We should expect that sapience now can develop and rapidly. The removal of the blinders allow us to see clearly. That may be the very definition of sapience.

The closest current representation of the naturalness of sapience is evident in the female gender. Even in women, it is still disrupted by the force of the men's aberrancy but it can still be distinguished in women. The disturbance is great and becoming more pronounced but so are the attempts by the women to overcome it.

Many, many women realize there is a problem and, in their lack of insight into the actual source of the problem, are fighting against it as best they can. The underlying sapience involved in those efforts to right our existence cannot be denied. They continue to attempt to make change in a loving manner. Women are the first place we should look for examples of sapience.

Love

Because of our blinders towards non-sentient sex, we missed the obvious. We can now begin to understand that, once all of the past strictures and false requirements concerning relationships were inspected, a couple living together in harmony is possible.

The most important relationship between humans can begin to thrive. Long term relationships can become the norm, once again, in a much more beneficial form than ever encountered in the past.

It has become just another accepted delusion that it is extremely unlikely that a relationship between a man and woman can last a lifetime in a contented state. Th prospect of relationships that not only last a lifetime but are a joy rather than a burden seems obvious. No longer the need to grin and bear it in misery.

With loving sex this can become the norm. The natural state, the only way in which stable relationships, leading to a stable humanity, will can begin.

The men will no longer change from being bright-eyed, bushy-tailed bundles of fun into a discouraging, grating individual utterly frustrated with life and his part in it. Men will no longer run from considering their physical failure in the relationship to pursue any other effort where they can have some remote chance at the missing feeling of success they so desire? Men can finally use much more discernment in their efforts and pursuits of life beyond the loving relationship between man and woman.

The typical rationales for the breakdown in relationships does not stand up to the least amount of rational scrutiny. This does. All aspects of a relationship can now succeed. Beyond that, the whole range of relationships between humans now have a chance at a symbiotic existence.

Love is important. Sentience enables the concept of love. Sentient sex permits the concept of love to prosper. It is the most important difference that can distinguish a truly sentience being. It is an intelligent, expanded form of caring that no other animal can ever achieve.

Sentient sex opens the way for succeeding at love on any scale from the relationships of a couple up to love of the human race for itself. Loving sex provides the underpinnings for this success. There is not a man alive that would rather go through life without ever satisfying his woman. That should no longer be a concern.

As the grip of love at the individual level begins to take full rein and unfettered sentience begins to emerge, the cultural effects will begin to be seen, as well. The ripple effects are straightforward.

Curiosity and questions. They are the two things that have gotten us this far, but the direction of our gaze has been limited in scope. Now that the bane of non-sentient sex has been revealed, it should no longer be hampered.

Resolution

When the whole of society finally recognizes and addresses the issues we have endured due to the appalling existence of non-sentient sex, mankind can finally begin to adopt the mantle of humanity as a sentient, loving, caring race. We will be ready to face anything that the universe throws at mankind.

The goodness of mankind

So far, mankind is perceived to be good only due to fear. Fear of god, fear of law and jail, fear of retribution, fear of others' perceptions. That is only because our natural state of goodness has been swindled up until this point in time. We need to recognize that being good is our natural state and has been obstructed by non-sentient sex. With the advent of loving sex, the emergence of mankind's goodness as a natural occurrence should happen of its own accord. The burr under the saddle of mankind will be gone.

We are currently propelled into that state of fear. Where does that fear come from? Some of it is a matter of the survival instinct and living for tens of thousands of years in a tenuous environment but a great deal of it certainly came from a foundation that was rocked to its core as each man began to believe that he was not a whole man and the woman was rocked by having to tolerate it. This produced a tendency towards paranoia, and enabler of fear of existence.

"Goodness", in the broadest terms, is as natural as breathing for an unencumbered human being. It is driven by fear in a forced situation. That situation should begin to alleviate, leaving mankind to show reveal its natural goodness.

Thoughtful evolution

We have, of course, been evolving our sentience for millennia with the greatest burst in that process in the last century, other than a short period approximately 3,000 years ago. The achievement of loving sex will be a significant stepping stone in that process. As our reason becomes unfettered, our progress should slow to a less frenetic pace as we learn to appreciate what we have, assess more diligently our path into the future, and begin to investigate what it means to be a truly sentient and sapient race. We can begin to question the motives behind so much that we do that is of questionable value, including some of our supposed progress. We can finally learn to begin to think before we act. We can move forward in a radically different, sane direction.

Acceptance

It is striking, as was discussed with various individuals in preparation of this book, that it really is the men that are more than willing to accept the situation as described in this book. Almost as if the removal of the blinders that have imposed was a serious relief - as long as there was a remedy. As if everyone was just waiting for someone else to say it, admit it. This shows clearly how close to the conscious mind the scourge exists and disrupts.

Men have always realized the disparity and recognized the discomfort at some fundamental level, just never wishing to recognize their own complicity in the situation until it is stated plainly and resolved. Of course, just the relief to realize that it is not their individual problem but a problem for the gender will be enormous. They understand the problem intimately because they lived through the nightmare of the burden.

Some men may be skeptical that there is a remedy, but it should prove itself out admirably. It is, also, extremely likely that some people will find it difficult getting over the perception that mankind is cursed and bad at heart and sex is terrible. If this happens, it will be those that have been treated most cruelly by the delusions and have lived with it the longest.

At one remove, women are more averse to accepting this. Women have lived through the debacle but not the first-hand experience of self-delusion and embarrassment. They just struggle to comprehend the significance of the burden or, like some men, cannot believe that the nightmare could possibly be over.

Of course, the conditioning that women is fraught with the idea that the best thing to do is just avoid the subject completely. Gun shy or the training that Pavlov's dog endured may describe it best. They seem to distrust the idea that the pain could finally be undone. Women will just be relieved when the unreason and disruption of men is finally eliminated. That is good enough.

For all, the very apparent difference between the general aberrancy of men and the general serenity of women should be clear. The change for men is at our doorstep. The end game is in sight.

Venus and Mars

Men take and women give is a good summary of the situation in which non-sentient sex is prevalent but it doesn't spell it out. The unacknowledged thread that lies below all of this is that men have not been holding up their part of the bargain, starting with the sexual exchange. This is changing with the more common acceptance of alternative means of bringing the woman to climax and that is certainly an improvement not to be ignored. In fact, it should be emphasized. In the absence of anything else working, go down on your woman. Of course, that is a vast improvement in comparison to the woman never reaching climax.

There still lies a problem, though. The woman is now completed to a much greater extent, but the man continues to feel incomplete through this method. Better than the past? Certainly. As good as it can get. Not even close.

The concept and explanations concerning men's and women's characteristics are incomplete. Neither has been seen in the full light of an existence including loving sex. This is, of course, due to the fact that we have yet to see what the two genders are like in a situation in which both are completed, sexually (women) as well as emotionally (men). It is likely that the two genders, in a world in which sexual satisfaction is the norm, will be starkly different than what exists today.

In many ways, the two genders are much more similar to each other than is the misperception in our current state of distortion. Many differences would be expected to remain between the two sexes, as well, but also, much more commonality. Most importantly, men will be able to finally shed the false appearances of manliness and replace it with humanity. Men will only need to retain the differences between the two genders that are truly natural and not due to forced distortions.

With their manhood assured, men can finally concentrate on something of substance. The assertion of their humanity and the characteristics of sentient love will be the most evident common traits, finally. Women are already much closer to this ideal. Venus and Mars will orbit closer than is currently the belief.

Ascendency

That lack of light, mentioned above, concerning the characteristics of men and women holds true for so many aspects of mankind itself, starting with sex. The bright, florescent light of sentience can now be turned on everything concerning humanity itself. The truth of humanity's existence can now be fully revealed with relief.

All of the pieces are now in place. Mankind can begin to ascend into integrated sentience and sapience. It is a huge turning point in humanity's existence. How quickly we can ascend will be dependent on how much of mankind's efforts can be brought to bear on removing the barriers to this ascendency. How willing will mankind be to admit to all of the misconceptions, conditioning and erroneous paradigms handed down by our ancient ancestors? It should be considered of paramount importance. Our balance needs to be restored.

What will it take and in what form will it begin to take shape? That would require a tremendous effort at scenario planning that does not fall into the context of this book.

Speculative predictions

It is impossible, though, after the immense time taken in studying this problem not to attempt some speculative predictions. These are not thoroughly vetted predictions. Consider it a sketch for a thorough scenario planning effort. It is just some sign posts to look for as we move forward to judge our progress and its veracity.

First thought that comes to mind is that the incessant need for input (or call it distraction) from outside sources, like the news, the internet, tv, etc may wane in the absence of the inner clamor of sexual dissatisfaction. In some ways, these could be considered just different forms of escapism. Some of them, like the news, almost ghoulish in nature. It is all like the most pervasive plague of escapism that ever existed.

We will no longer need the noise to block out the uncomfortable feelings of existence. We may be able to replace much of the incessant noise with the soothing music of our existence.

Human interaction should be expected to become much more prevalent. Human interaction has been curbed in all its forms by the specter of non-sentient sex and the feelings of unworthiness it supplies. It has affected, in particular, the man's view of any interaction considerably.

The isolation can become inclusion.

As well, we will no longer need to encumber ourselves with the baggage of many of our past mistakes.   Many, many of the mistakes should reveal themselves in short order.   Many of the secondary and tertiary behaviour mechanisms should fall by the wayside naturally with little or no effort.   Many more will be revealed for the mishaps they are through conscious effort.

A rapid change in the social structure that has existed under the burden of non-sentient sex for so long seems very likely.   Just like a horse that has been restrained by a bit for so long finally finds itself unleashed or a body of water that is no longer restrained by a dam or a keylog.   The flood of affection could be something delightful to observe as it unfolds.

Certainly, it is to be expected that the finer qualities of mankind will come to the fore.   The finer qualities of mankind will finally come to the fore.   The finer qualities, such as honour, dignity, respect, and courtesy can become commonplace and not something that is only forced through peer pressure. They are a natural evolutionary path for a sentient species that has conquered the many encumbrances endured by animals.

The baser qualities of mankind, such as brutishness and bullying will be more easily recognized as the shameful, distorted animalistic characteristics that they are and wane to insignificance.   These will be characteristics that an individual, no longer in the shadow of non-sentient sex, will be unwilling to portray.   The baser qualities of mankind will become unacceptable on the individual basis (most importantly) and unaccepted in all of society.   The concept of alpha male will be seen as the brute adaptation it is.

We will transform humanity into a caring race, more intent on making existence a proper situation for all of mankind rather than something endured by many.   The insanity of mankind will be effortlessly replaced by sapience and clarified sentience.

Such things as politeness, in fact, should become an effortless mainstay rather than a matter of diplomacy.   Political correctness is the subjugated form of politeness.   It is a forced situation among cultures disturbed by the disrupted characteristics of sexually inept men for the purposes of keeping the peace (or, more exactly, avoiding outbreaks of unreason and violence) rather than an outgrowth of serenity and caring.

We are human, sentient.

The real expectation is that the shackles that bind us will not just be loosened, they will shattered completely.

The best prediction for the future can be summarized in a single word. Celebration. Of existence, of being human.

Background material and justification

This chapter is a lot of information that was necessary in developing these insights, as well as corroborative information for the arguments.

Behavioural mechanisms

Everyone of us is affected by that which surrounds us. While there may be discussion as to the importance of nature versus nurture, there can be no doubt that events that impinge on a person affect who they are. As an extreme example, putting the concept to the test of limits, the loss of an arm or leg would influence a person's character, for better or for worse.

Those events can be termed behavioural influences or mechanisms. A pebble in the shoe is a pedestrian example (groan). The pain or discomfort encountered from a pebble in the shoe will affect the way one walks, and more than likely, one's mood. The pebble can be considered a behavioural mechanism.

The strength of influence of any particular behavioural mechanism varies depending on the importance of that mechanism's affect on one's self-image. If a large pebble stays in the shoe such that it causes pain, it is certain to affect one's walk, and further, over a considerable period of time, one's mood and perspective on life. It will hardly be ignored. It may harden the person to struggle through the pain, or find a way to avoid the pain, or adapt to the pain, or be consumed by the distraction, but it cannot be ignored.

A feeling of despair, whether brought on by constant induced pain or from constant disappointment in life, will drastically affect one's self image and outlook. There will be a ripple effect into all aspects of one's life if it is a significant disappointment. How common the occurrence is within the population tells how much of an effect it has on society as a whole.

Some of the most powerful behavioural mechanisms are those which are encountered before the mind has developed to the stage of discrimination and critical thinking. When a child is first developing, there is no discrimination. All inputs are accepted at face value without any reasonable degree of questioning or critique.

This is especially true of input provided by those closest to the person, the role models by which one shapes their thoughts and future selves. Especially when those thoughts are conveyed as irrefutable. Whether those role models are adults, an older child, or a peer, the effects are the same. (As a sidebar, consider the significance and importance that women, in the past, have been of primary family member involved in raising children and influencing the child's development and just thank our lucky stars it has been so! If not, we might have been up to our knees in blood).

This early, unquestioning acceptance leads to paradigms that, as insane as they may be, become the centerpiece of that person's view of life. The influence of these fundamentally accepted principles of life have life-long consequences.

As a simple example, if that child is repeatedly called stupid by all of those closest to the child, then it is a fair bet that child will perceive itself as stupid and become, for all intents and purposes, stupid. Or, if that child gains the perspective of being inherently better or more valuable than others, the child will go through life considering others of less value as human beings.

These are the mechanisms that set the stage for a person's life. Even though these are outside influences, they are so deeply intertwined with the person's perceptions, without the facility of critical thinking having intervened, that they are nearly impossible to remove and are mostly accepted as fundamental principles of life not open to argument. The later development of critical thinking has difficulty scrutinizing the conditioning done before its advent.

Later in life, one will encounter behavioural mechanisms that attempt to influence a person's perceptions. A boss that attempts to instill subjugation through fear. A friend that would like to influence one into believing changing one's view on something. At this stage, once the discriminatory faculty is fully developed, as well as a set of beliefs based on earlier accepted principles, the result becomes much more dependent on previously developed views.

Many of those that embrace critical thinking as a way of life never even suspect that much of their over-reaction is based on attempts to purge the conditioning done before their discriminatory facility was developed.

The more constant and abiding the mechanism, the more influence it will have. A person that tolerates the boss attempting to instill subjugation will slowly be transformed. Whether the person being affected begins to resemble a slave, an angry person, or has little effect depends in large part on those earliest influences and current environment.

it takes a significant event to have a serious effect after the critical faculties are developed. A traumatic experience, for instance. This can disorient a person considerably. If it is repeated regularly, it can unhinge.

Conditioned to failure

There is so much conditioning that is picked up from the very fabric of our lives, throughout our existence, that is seldom even recognized.

The same aspects of behavioural mechanisms hold true for societies and humanity as a whole. Consider the insidious phrase that embraces so succinctly all of the defeatist attitude and conditioning embraced by mankind concerning humanity itself. "We're only human." We're only human??!!? This phrase is usually accepted without a blink of the eye. We are the most magnificent creature in existence! This defeatist attitude is so saturated into our existence that we don't even question it.

There is some unrecognized bane, some hidden disruptor that encourages our destructive, violent tendencies and our willingness to accept this state of affairs.

This acceptance of failure as a natural trait of our species is so drilled into us that we accept all of the inane behaviours that surround us. There is one element that validates this belief. The phrases of abnegation justify themselves because of a single massive failure on the part of humans and the resultant conditioning that reduces us. It no longer needs to exist. The phrases of renunciation of humanity's goodness and capabilities will dissipate like the fog they cause once the root cause is removed.

The root cause, the behavioural mechanism at the heart of it all is the disorienting effects of non-sentient, disconcerting sex. The resultant unreason is the downfall. It is significant, traumatic and repeated regularly in so many individuals that it completely disrupts humanity's existence.

While the worst effects develop well after the critical thinking faculty has been developed as we progress past pubescence, the stage is already set by the unwittingly absorbed deception that everything is normal and sex should be nothing short of wonderful. Even this instilled belief is bent into contortions by the often absorbed belief, *most often in tandem with the belief that sex is nothing short of wonderful,* that sex is cursed, unnatural, and bad. The emphasis put on these two disparate beliefs during a person's childhood can also be contemplated to understand further the differences between how people perceive and adapt to the later presence of their sexual nature. Do you begin to see the utterly ridiculous, confusing situation in which mankind exists as it pertains to sex???

It is a certainty that it will drastically impinge on the feelings of self-respect for the individual and the species. It is one of the most persistent mechanisms in existence, once a person reaches puberty. For many, it is the slow, subconsciously dawning realization that things were not as portrayed, thus disrupting the foundations on which a life was built.

The fact that this terribly disabling deception takes place *after* the critical faculties have been developed makes the impact and import of the initial self-deception just that much more devastating. It insinuates its way through the rational and critical facilities subjugating and crippling them for the rest of a lifetime. If much emphasis was put on the curse of sex, then not only are the faculties compromised by faulty reasoning but also undermined by a belief system that can lead to rack and ruin.

The earlier absorbed belief that there is nothing to be learned about sex beyond where to stick it, that sex is wonderful without any special effort, amplifies the unfortunate consequences in the stability of the foundations of that person. There must be something wrong with the person since sexual intercourse is not the wonderful event expected.

Or, as may be the case for a very oblivious man, that the experience is everything he desires, while he remains oblivious to the fact that the woman is not experiencing the same pleasure. In this case, it may come as a complete surprise when the woman develops a lack of interest or desires to move on.

The bones of your body, just like the thoughts and paradigms from non-sentient sex, become bent in compensation to the painful pebble and the adjustments made to movement. The relief from the removal of the pebble is tremendous and the effect is more pronounced for a younger person that hasn't had his whole life bent by the presence of that pebble in the shoe.

It does not really seem possible that an older person who has carried the burden of non-sentient sex for many decades can ever really completely recover, psychologically. Too many habits of thought have been conceived, too many disruptive behavioural mechanisms have been encountered. They will at least leave scars. They may be assuaged, there will certainly be tremendous relief but many, many paradigms have had their effect. Still, the relief of sexual adequacy, or even just the knowledge that one is not alone in one's struggle, will be more than compensatory at any point in life.

Without the conscious awareness of the problem, it undermines everything in humanity's existence. Just like anything else that begins to have an effect in a person's life, the reaction is based on past events and learnings.

At the level that non-sentient sex saturates society, it also must be recognized to have behavioural effects at the cultural level. Anything that is common across a society, such as a religion, government, television and news programming (good word) influences and modifies the society's behaviour. The biggest difference being that there are zero boundaries within humanity to non-sentient sex. It crosses all strata of society, all countries borders, and all religions.

At some point in the distant past, many millennia ago, aberrant behavioural mechanisms, in the form of the conditioning of humanity by humanity, began to develop as commonly accepted beliefs. These damaging behavioural mechanisms that dealt with the inconsistencies forced on sentient humanity by non-sentient sex began to assert themselves. That it infiltrated every aspect of life (e.g. misogyny) across the globe shows that recognition of the bane existed long before religions or governments were developed. The way in which different religions deal with the topic of sex shows one of the first divergences in the area of non-sentient sex.

The dawning realisation of non-sentient sex by men distorted humanity towards brutality and unreason by creating stories to justify their lack and furthered our fall. These stories became embedded in every utterance. The temptress, the bearer of evil, all have the markings of the aberrant attitude and delusions due to men's failings at sex.

The inadequacy, invariably, leads to feelings of inferiority and frustration. How could it be otherwise? Misogyny could be considered a cultural level compensation behavioural mechanism, as can the erroneous caricature of manliness, due to the pervasiveness of the problem.

Secondary and tertiary mechanisms

Unreason becomes the outlet of the root behavioural mechanism of non-sentient sex. It is portrayed in many forms. Unreasoning anger and aggression, disillusionment and withdrawal from life, as well as irrational opinions and lifestyles are among the most common. These are all passed on to children from the role models of adults.

The root cause of these forms that unreason takes is well masked by the secondary and tertiary behavioural mechanisms that developed due to the initial root cause complicating the landscape drastically. The fact that this most enduring, constantly reinforced behavioural mechanism occurs in the already developed consciousness once pubescence arrives just makes the slow realization that much more traumatic as it conflicts with the earlier embedded uncritically accepted beliefs or reinforces the belief that sex is bad, cursed. The upheaval caused by both combined can leave a person at a complete loss.

No sign of the coming trouble is visible before pubescence (unless through role models), so it begins to creep up on a person's life like a thief in the night because the expectation is non-existent and the reality is too much to bear. It takes years to completely unmask itself, if it ever does. The many and varied responses, in the form of secondary and tertiary mechanisms, are like ripples in a pond continually expanding from this single, seemingly insurmountable difficulty of inept sexual intercourse. The closer the response is related to sex, the more obvious the connection. All of the common sexual perversions of men are the most obvious of all.

Many secondary and tertiary behavioural mechanisms that pervade all of human society are a result of the distortions introduced by inadequate sexual ability. The relentless subconscious realization and inability to accept the inadequacy causes these aberrant feelings and reactions to begin within the individual, just as the pebble causes compensation to the way one walks and functions. Already existing and accepted mechanisms, such as misogyny, are adopted when available due to the ease of adoption.

Our suppression of the topic of sex over the millennia has made it a perfect breeding ground for aberrant and obsessive behaviours.   The accompanying, deceptive assumptions and folk tales regarding the subject, as well as the more official pontifications developed to explain away the issue just exacerbate the situation. These were just the first forays of unreason that now have traveled far from the original topic and have enabled all of the delusions of the race. While many of the behaviours are far removed from the topic of sex, they are all due to the underlying unreason caused by non-sentient sex. This explains the extreme difficulty in recognizing the source problem, the root cause.

The manipulation and suppression of women globally, in the form of misogyny, is clear unreason.   That the purpose was to promote feelings of superiority in men in the face of men's abject failure at sex fits the situation perfectly. In fact, if you look at the conversation of humanity on the subject of misogyny, there is never any reference to the source of this horrendous behaviour on the part of mankind. It is not even openly mentioned that the obvious and only possible source of misogyny is men!

Men being the only possible source of the issue is blatant. Why in the world would men want to do this? It is treated as if it were just some natural occurrence, like the tides, not something created by half of humanity.   Its existence is just accepted, just as the phrase 'we're only human' is accepted. If this doesn't surprise you then you are still deep in the thralls of non-sentient sex.

The irrationality of the development of misogyny within an intelligent, sentient race is so apparent that we should have always been looking for the source. That the existence of misogyny is accepted by the human race as an expected outcome of our earliest existence is so far gone into delusion and irrationality as to be completely breathtaking. Why on earth would a developing sentient race become misogynistic? Why on earth would half of the human race be relegated to the status of cattle?

That it needs to be 'fixed' rather than obliterated from our behavioural patterns is blatantly misguided. It makes no sense at all ... except for a single reason. It only makes sense in the context of the rest of men's behavioural patterns. When taken together into consideration, the arrow points only one way. The reaction to non-sentient sex, that blinds us to so much irrationality in our day-to-day activities, is the only viable reason for the suppression of women that has gone on far too long.

It is a dimwitted behaviour, along with many others, initiated by our ancient ancestors for which there has never been any valid, supportable purpose at all. Legislation can never entirely resolve the issue of misogyny. The best it can ever do is *attempt* to put a cap on it. Unfortunately, even those efforts would lead to their own harm for humanity in almost certainly exacerbating the war between the sexes without the resolution provided by loving sex and sentient love. With those two, of course, there is no need for legislation.

Ironically, women really could be satisfied, to some extent, with just the considerations of holding and caring, it seems. They do not have the overriding requirement of sex on a regular basis nor the overriding urge for sexual satisfaction. This does not provide a resolution, though, because the man does have that overriding urge. If the woman is not satisfied by the act, in the absence of that overriding urge, why would she have the same desire to have sex regularly? It is certainly an setup for failure of the man-woman relationship if the woman is not satisfied. It is also certainly a loss, in and of itself, if women are not satisfied. While the woman can reach some level of satisfaction in life without the completion provided by satisfying sexual relations, make no mistake, it enables another level of satisfaction with life for both that completes them and the human race.

The behavioural mechanism of seeking alternative sexual lifestyles is also a distortion attempting to compensate for the lack of sexual adequacy. This is just another strong justification for mankind to grow up and realize that sex should be good for both the man and the woman.

It became clear during the investigations (decades, in all) that cultures are really just one huge behavioural mechanism, from which a society operates, based on conditioning that leads to habits of thought that encourages certain views and behaviours while curtailing others. So far, the cultural level behavioural mechanisms have been haphazard, at best, leading mankind with no apparent purpose, and certainly, little reason. It is a near certainty that, for a reasoning, fully sentient race, the behavioural mechanisms developed in a culture could become a powerful tool for the advancement of civilization, something that has eluded us due to our distraction and bewilderment.

Breaking through the inadvertent behavioural methods and paradigms conditioned into humanity is the final step towards becoming truly human. The first is ridding ourselves of the destruction of self-respect at the individual level due to the disruptive nature of non-sentient sex.

Scenarios

This is looking at a number of current scenarios that are continuously repeated between couples within the context of our current situation. There are many scenarios that play out within the boundaries of non-sentient sexual relationships brought on by differences in conditioning (both from childhood and ongoing assessment of the existing conditions), situation, and mindset.

The complications

Of course, everything concerning non-sentient sex is complicated or difficult which is probably why this root cause of our unreason could hide so easily for so long in plain sight.   Maybe it was because we were so busy surviving.   Maybe it was required to be as such for the human race to survive to this point.   That is no longer a concern.   What is now required is intelligence, sapience, reason, and loving relationships at the individual level.   What is now a concern is that we become sane, completely sentient, and truly sapient in light of our abundance of knowledge and very dangerous capabilities.

If one thinks about it, this is the only way it could ever work.   One can't decree love at the cultural level any more than one can decree peace.   It has to be driven by relationships between individuals that work, from the ground up.   A more loving culture should be expected as the end result.   We need this far more desperately than the next widget.   This is exactly what is wrong with just about everything we attempt today to improve the situation.   It is always a forced solution.   We implement laws to force people to "be good".   It could never work well.   It was a fumbling, non-sentient attempt at improving conditions.   It was attempting to use outside forces to remove the surface issues rather than recognizing that something was wrong at the very heart of humanity that provided the distortions to sentience and the eliminated any potential to eventually achieve sapience.   Sapience could never be expected under such conditions.   The most important relationship that must work before any other could really work was the relationship between couples.

There are a wide variety of ways in which people adapt to the slow realization over a lifetime of sexual dissatisfaction.   It is that important to the self-image and all aspects of human consciousness.

The individual consciousness will, of course, find some way to cope with this distressful situation and these are the scenarios that our lives tend to follow, depending on the conditions.   The consciousness will always find some way to rationalize existence, even if it drives it to irrational perceptions of existence.

Only those lucky few that have stumbled upon true sexual adequacy and satisfaction for both themselves and their Lady through sexual intercourse avoid this fundamental disturbance completely and have a chance to arrive at a rational scenario for their existence.   The other scenarios played out are all too familiar and the results have, so far, been completely disastrous, confusing, unremitting, and disappointing because of the distortions that kept us from recognizing non-sentient sex.

Personality change

Sentience changes everything. Most of all, it changes men, which is something that many, many women have experienced. The complete change in personality of the man. He starts out extremely loving, and caring, considering the woman's every wish or pleasing in whatever manner works for the woman. Then something happens. Over time (or overnight), the man begins to withdraw and become someone that is nearly unrecognizable. What is at the heart of it?

The dawning in the man that he is not being manly in the sexual arena, along with the normal circumstances of life begin to wear on the man. He becomes aware, at some level, that he is not sexually adequate. He begins to feel emasculated. The various responses from this suppressed realization are as varied as there are men that struggle with the situation.

None of the responses have the remotest possibility of being rational due to the underlying irrationality of the situation. Even though the woman may be relatively content, it really doesn't matter. He know he's not doing what is necessary to ring the woman's chime. If he is at least free enough of constraints as to find some other way to satisfy his woman sexually or, if the woman is tolerant of the minimization of satisfaction (not a recommendation), he may dodge the worst components of this disappointment. What else could cause such a radical change in a man's personality that so very many women have experienced it firsthand? The game-playing this can cause to confuse and obfuscate the issue are another matter entirely.

Case study

This is a case study of what is almost certain to happen when a man does not satisfy a woman and the ramifications to the individuals involved.

A man begins having sex without realizing that he lacks the ability to sexually satisfy a woman without some additional effort. In most cases, he has been told little more than "stick it in".

The ensuing thought process he follows is nearly unavoidable, if he continues to pursue sex with the opposite gender. A rationalization is almost certain to take place.

As he cannot find a way to satisfy her, then he must find a way to come to terms with this as a sentient being. That is unavoidable. If he cannot learn to assure her satisfaction in some way, he is inadvertently saying to himself (and her) that her satisfaction is of no importance. It does not matter that this happens inadvertently, that it can't be avoided. He must come to terms with the situation. It does not matter that the man feels there is no alternative. It is like drowning in a pool of quicksand. The mental state, as well as the emotional attachment, will suffer. The self-image requires some response. As noted earlier, the exception of finding some other way to satisfy the woman is the next best alternative and relieves a great deal of the disturbance mentioned below but does not completely resolve the issue.

In essence, if he does not find some way to satisfy her, he is beginning to say that she is not as important as he is. In essence, he is saying she is not worth the effort. Even though that is not the man's intent, the requirement of an integrated self-image requires that some internal response, rationale, and explanation is given to define the situation. This may be where the concept that sex was a curse initiated. It was felt to be the inevitable conclusion, since sexual ineptitude seemed to be the unavoidable result.

The end result is the thought process that the woman's satisfaction is not worth the effort or that it is her fault. While finding some other way to satisfy the woman certainly improves the situation, it does only a little to improve the man's self-image. He has still not proved to himself that he can satisfy the woman by lasting long enough to do so during coitus as is the sentient expectation. This certainly affects the man's feelings of masculinity. If he has the wit to realize that this is the common state of affairs with men, his self-respect will suffer the least and his rationalizations will be minimized. Keep in mind that any thought of needing to satisfy the woman's sexual being is a recent occurrence. Up until recent times, the whole concept of a woman's sexual satisfaction was not often a consideration that was entertained. Even today, it is the exception for many men, in many parts of the world to consider his woman's satisfaction of importance - at a conscious level.

This thought process is not acknowledged by the conscious mind, which makes the mental disturbance terribly insidious. All of these ruminations initially take place at a subconscious level. They influence the thought processes often without ever being acknowledged consciously or intentionally adopted because the rational mind knows they are deceits.

When they are, finally, merged into the conscious mind, there are only the slightest remnants of its origin. All that is left is an inferiority complex, a self-centeredness, and a disdain for women.

The woman's path through the maze is, of course, radically different. In some ways, her maze of conditioning has been built to hide any mention or recognition of the original problem. It may lead to utter frustration and despair from which the woman is very likely to think that there is something wrong with her or just complete bafflement at the throes of existence.

The woman, not being driven by the destruction of her self-respect, does not as easily become disturbed. In recent times, though, with less desire for children due to the population pressure and economic realities, the woman flounders more, also. It takes a rare woman indeed, to realize the actual source of the problem. Current sociological pressures, along with the often lacking recognition that there is even a problem for the man, make it very unlikely that she will ever blame the man.

One end result for the man is some level of misogyny. Maybe it is undeclared but it most often lurks in the background. To the woman, the end result is insecurity and complete bafflement concerning this aspect of life. The man's baffling conduct does not help. It only deepens the mystery and misery for the woman.

The only real solution is true, face-to-face loving sex with pleasure for both. There is nothing that can match sexual intercourse for sexual pleasure and reinforcing the emotional aspects of love from a physical standpoint. Without it, the emotional aspects are besieged and disrupted, if not destroyed. Any way in which to satisfy your partner, though, goes a long ways towards alleviating the feelings of lack of self-worth.

A baffling and disappointing scenario

One scenario is the man who spends a single night with a woman and always moves on, pursuing the woman until his inept ability at sexual intercourse brings the whole facade crashing down on his head with that particular woman. He moves on. He cannot face his own failure and he knows it at some subliminal level. He may not admit it, but deep in his heart, he knows it, otherwise he wouldn't move on. The sexual drive and the desperate need to feel that he can find someone with whom he can feel satisfactory will drive him for years.

He is so fascinating and self-assured before the event. Even he doesn't really understand it. He just walks away with this terribly disappointed feeling after the perceived debacle and cannot face his self-image, or the woman, under those conditions. His personal situation is assured to deteriorate as time, and his failures, progress.

It is nearly impossible for him to believe he is doing something wrong at one of the most basic activities in existence. How could that possibly be? The whole situation baffles him completely.

It may take an inordinately long time for him to come to the realization of what is really wrong late in his life. Much more likely is that he continues the easier route of self-deception, misery, and self-destruction that emanates throughout all of his interactions. Even the mid-life crisis comes and goes without recognition.

Each time he tries, he is often hoping that he can finally find someone that he can satisfy without the thought ever entering his consciousness that his is the failure, a deception on its own.

Like Pavlov's dog, the repeated cruelty of the situation, due to his seeking the ultimate pleasure but having it fall to ashes repeatedly, will continue to wear on him, leading to complete disappointment in life.

It is the precise reason that this man reaches mid-life crisis. At some deep and fundamental level, he realizes that things are not as they seem. Because of the conditioning nonsense of a lifetime, he can never pin it down to non-sentient sex. Because he has been convinced that it is just the way it is (all you need to do is stick it in!), he will never even consider that it can be different. He may very well fear exactly that. That, if he does not find a woman that he can satisfy, then all is lost, because he will not get better at it.

Make no mistake, there is surely an inkling at first, at least at a subconscious level that may or may not finally begin to become clear at some later point in his life: it is his failure. It just becomes increasingly evident and disturbing over a lifetime, as the failures to satisfy continue to mount, providing a crushing blow to the self-image. Thus, mid-life crisis.

It really doesn't matter that the woman is feeling like everything was alright or that the sex would get better with time. He knows it's not and he knows it won't.

The existing rationale says that he is a jerk. That really doesn't explain anything. The missing nail does. He may or may not become a jerk in all aspects of life but there is a source for the behavioural disturbance that can be removed. He is misled by the distortion just as everyone down the centuries has been. The cruelest part of the deception starts with himself.

This is a man who is failing at sexual intercourse and cannot face it at all. It is just too unbelievable and unbearable. How can it be that an individual cannot succeed at the most fundamental activity of life?

He is confident that he adores women and pursues them vigorously up until the crushing disappointment of sexual intercourse throws his perceived failure, once again, in his face and he cannot face or comprehend the failure. He moves on.

It most likely never dawns on him that the common animal has no need to satisfy its mate. Both of the participants of the lower order of animals being completely driven by the unrelenting forces of nature unembellished by sentience, sapience, and reason just don't care. In the embellished state of humanity, his failure distorts or destroys all three. Only mankind must finally go beyond the mere rutting. The beauty is that sex for humans can become something transcendent. Reason and celebration should rule rather than the absence of it.

A modern scenario

Another scenario that is more likely today, as alternatives are accepted, is the slow withdrawal from society and interaction with those of the opposite sex as disappointment and the feeling of helplessness gain a foothold. The inundation of information and media accelerates (and continues to distort) the knowledge that something is not right. It often no longer needs to wait for a midlife crisis. A quiet desperation becomes prevalent with the only easy, though less than satisfying, relief being the less than perfect satisfaction of self-stimulation. A quiet desperation where he hides from the world. This is more and more possible, and therefore, likely scenario in today's world.

Common scenarios

Of course, there are the most common occurrences. All cases involving marriage or long term relationships. The longest term relationships, nowadays, happen after the individual has been brutalized by non-sentient sex long enough to realize that it's not going to change. The best hope is just to find someone else that is willing to accept the inevitable defeat.

In general, unless the man discovers how to extend the time of his erection during sexual intercourse and is, thus, able to actually continue to enhance the care and cherishing for his Lady and the enabling life affirmation of their relationship, the situation is as regular as the sunrise.

The normal route

The man wants sex regularly. The woman begins the relationship feeling the same way. Then, as time passes, the woman loses interest. She loses interest because she is not getting the same transcendent experience. She also does not experience the same overwhelming urge as the man to repeat the experience that the burden of semen building up causes and the lack of satisfaction, on her part, impedes.

This does not imply that a woman is incapable of ongoing enthusiasm concerning sex, which seems to be the normal assumption. The common comment that it is just not that important for her is misleading. It is not important if she does not experience the best of it. One wonders about the effect on a woman that just knows how wonderful orgasms are but can never find it with a mate.

It's just that the necessary pleasure that she should be enjoying is missing. Her only overriding urge instilled by nature is to have children but it is not the only overriding satisfaction that she can attain.

Since sex is not the overriding physical joy that it should be for the woman, she loses interest. The man, assuredly, never loses interest.

The couple marries in total emotional bliss. Then, the years wear away the emotional bliss due to the physical frustrations and disparity caused by non-sentient sex. This is where the scenarios diverge.

Grin and bear it alternative

One scenario is that the two each decide that things are good enough and going out to find someone else would be too much trouble and probably wouldn't change anything that much. This is usually a couple that have gone through multiple relationships and recognize that what they desire will just never happen. Sad to say that, in the past, they were right. This is the couple that faces the actual, evident reality fairly well and deals with the world as it is with aplomb.

This is the couple that accepts a life of limitations. It may often be mired in the midst of misery and disappointment wearing away at both the physical and emotional aspects of their relationship across a lifetime. It is sad indeed, but one must respect those involved in such a scenario in the absence of understanding of the actual situation and the actual potential bliss.

The woman becomes less and less interested in sex, since there is no benefit in the activity for her. She may find other interest and is least affected by the absence of the most pleasurable experience in life. She may even continue feigned interest in sex. A child or children may distract her for most of twenty years to keep the disappointment at bay. If the woman does not find a way to continue tolerating sex regularly and often, then the man struggles daily with the lack of sexual release in some way but carries on.

The main impact on both is the deterioration of the emotional satisfaction from the closest possible relationship.

The man, also, may find other interests to distract himself. The man may withdraw into himself. The level of anger and unreason in that man tells much about how often he finds some form of release.

This is the main scenario that mankind has followed for ages though, lately, the alternatives have been coming to the fore.

The breakup alternative

Another scenario is when one or both realizes, consciously, that something is wrong, even though it is unlikely that they realize what exactly is wrong. As our sentience emerges more and more, this is becoming a more common occurrence. One or both find the situation intolerable and are unwilling to continue to accept it. Note that this may be the same people as in the scenario above that have just not accepted the miserable conclusion, yet, that sex will just never be good. That may change in the next relationship.

From here, there are many variations. One of the couple thinks there must be something wrong with their spouse or that they have become "incompatible" or have "irreconcilable differences", so looks for someone new. It is a grasping at straws. The person finds a new mate and the disappointment is repeated, and sooner or later, they accept the inevitable disappointment of life, finally marrying someone for the second, third, or more times and accepting what seems inevitable. As the man's sexual drive become less urgent, this scenario almost works. At its best, it is still far from the best possibility of celebration of life.

Of course, there may be other reasons for incompatibility in some marriages, but until the bane of non-sentient sex no longer clouds the issue for the human race, it will be difficult to distinguish the reality.

Another one of the accepted states of affair that the distortion has made seem so natural is the desire for "something new". That "something new" may seem more exciting or may seem to hold more promise. To some, those that are convinced that they are no more than an animal, this will seem natural. It is in essence, a form of that unending fount of hope at the bottom of Pandora's box. It allows for the stirrings of desire, once again. People shrug off the disappointment in the situation and try again ... and again ... and again. Missing the key component, the struggle continues unabated.

The younger model

Can you now see the insanity of this deception and its source? A man, with the subconscious realization that his sexual stamina is not all that it should be, may decide that young women are great. Younger women that have not learned to distinguish inept sexual intercourse and still hold out for the false hope that they will somehow, some way, sometime enjoy satisfactory sex are easy prey. That is such a deviance from an honest approach to life that it should be self-evident, and hopefully, in the near future, will be. A resounding echo of that first deceit that cripples a man's ability to be human.

The historical view of this is that it's just the way it is, young women attract all men. While there is surely some truth to this, the underlying truth is that young women are inexperienced and may not really know what it means to be sexually satisfied and have not become jaded and disappointed with the search for such. The nubile beauty is paltry compared to a shared lifetime.

This model is a refutation of mankind as a higher life-form and a complete dismissal of the caring and personal relationship that should be expected to grow from such caring. The naiveté of young women makes them a prime target for men who are sexually inadequate. The women won't know what they are missing, so that man is safe, for a few years, until she does. Then, he just moves on to his next disappointment in life.

This may also, sadly, teach the young woman the ways to substitute for a caring, personal, endearing relationship. That money, power, and fame can be an attractive substitute in the absence of sexual pleasure. Flaunting a beautiful body for the idiot men that are so deluded as to think that is what it is all about.

Validation

Another prime scenario that leads to many sub-scenarios is led by the delusions concerning love. This is not meant to disavow love. Quite the opposite, in fact. It is meant to clarify what is not love but some distortion of the reality induced by non-sentient sex.

The scenario is the one that many men and women follow in their earliest pursuits of a satisfying self-image. The young, quite often, seek validation of their self-image in others. This is certain to be, at least, partially driven by the inadequacy (insecurity?) concerning mankind's sexual capabilities. They do not recognize it as such.

It is something that is instilled by the lack of surety that they sensed from their parents and/or role models. What else could rock the foundations of an adult, leading to feelings of insecurity more than the feeling of sexual inadequacy? The young explore the subject of sex with insecurity and awkwardness, long before they ever encounter the ineptness of the current sexual landscape because they are primed for trouble in a vague, undefined way by role models.

The desperate attempts to find someone, anyone, that will *accept* them reveals the truth. The irrationality of this pursuit will become less common as the scourge of non-sentient sex becomes apparent to all and is eliminated.

A person needs to be confident in themselves first, completely happy with the self-image that is reflected in the mirror of their mind, before there is the slightest chance that love and caring for someone else can fully develop. Love is not a refuge, it is a celebration and fulfillment that can only be attained in the presence of loving sex. It should be as natural as the sunrise.

Categories

Once a man realizes that he is not sexually satisfying his female partner, there are a number of behavioural scenarios that can be expected. One scenario is that some men may attempt to convince themselves that it's the woman's fault and play mind games to continue to have sex.

This case can often lead to verbal, emotional, and all too often, physical violence to assure that he gets sex. If nothing else, it will involve mind and dominance games that are not fulfilling to life. All of this happens far too often in some cultures. This further insanity may often be caused by a subconscious fear that his secret is out or may be ruminating in the woman's mind. This is most often combined with the fact that the woman's enthusiasm, if not willingness, wanes. Blaming it on the woman is an easy, though insane rationale and excuse to delve no further into the subject.

Unfortunately, the opposite is also true way too often. The woman feels responsible. That she is doing something wrong. That guilt that women are conditioned to accept must have occurred over the ages as a result of the mind games and physical abuse just mentioned. What is a near instinctual reaction of guilt shows just how far and just how long this ridiculous situation has been present. The woman is never responsible as long as a man cannot find a way to sexually satisfy her.

There are those men that may just fall back on a lifetime of self-stimulation as the primary sexual release. There are those that decide to attract women through some other means, such as money, power, or prestige, casting the women aside as soon as it seems their sexual inadequacy is becoming apparent, relegating the woman to little more than a sex toy.

In many cases, it works out much like the mistress. The woman gains a financial settlement that equates to a similar situation. If the woman can convince the man that she is content and salve the man's feelings of emasculation, it may last a lifetime. Many societies seem to accept this as the norm. In essence, that is the unspoken reason for the current divorce setup. Give the woman lots of money. She earned it!

In some culture, it seems much more accepted that men are terrible at sex. The wives have little to do with sex other than to bear children and the men find other women, that are paid for the service.

Most often, in all of these cases, the men may never have a conscious clue as to their sexual inadequacy, but still, they compound the problem through obsessive and aberrant pursuits in the absence of loving sex, making them less compatible with anyone: mate, colleague, acquaintance, or barista.

There are those that just visit prostitutes whenever they feel the urge. Then, it is just a straight-up transaction with no emotional involvement. Both get what they want and no one need be deluded.

The man that can dally casually with many women is not likely to continue in this new light. It is not truly satisfying, except on a physical basis. The physical satisfaction accompanied by the emotional satisfaction and the deep history of sharing between two individuals is the most rewarding of all. Anything less is a compromise.

Rather than promoting promiscuity, loving sex is likely to encourage more permanent, definitive mating. For both, the satisfaction and reinforcement of self-image brought on by loving sex would impede the need (and insanity) of seeking elsewhere. All of the delusions and less than satisfactory scenarios are the victims of a distorted, unhappy self-image.

It is the incessant feeling of inadequacy, along with the increasingly apparent lack of interest from his lady and the accompanying lack of sex, that drives some men (and women) into seeking sex elsewhere.

Secondly, the emotional bond between men and women should not fray nearly as easily as before, reinforcing the unlikelihood of either straying.

The desperate attempts to seek someone's approval and masking it as love should diminish greatly. Confidence in one's own self-image would rule out the need.

Of course, other things should be expected as well. As an example, the very bizarre notion of pornography should finally fade away, as well as the awful notion of the sex trade and all other aberrations involving sex. To say it will be a new day for mankind, may be an understatement in the extreme. Only time will tell for certain.

Aberrations and obsessions

The major complication in discerning the effects of sexual inadequacy on a person's character is that the personality, and very probably the career path and level of success, is well-defined before the first hint of concern about sexual inadequacy impinges on a man.

Non-sentient sex is completely counter to a man's expectations and is cushioned by society's underlying structure built to repress any inkling of sexual inadequacy of the male. More so, in the past, it was built to compensate for his lack. An utterly non-sentient disaster. This means that the man is most likely to be completely blind-sided by the situation. Without the identification and recognition of the situation and the techniques and considerations that can alleviate the condition, the delusion continues.

The end result, though, is, in effect, always the same. A growing despondency about life, in one form or another, due to non-sentient sex that is revealed in any of a number of destructive traits to oneself and/or others.

The way in which those traits are expressed vary widely because the preconditions of one's life are well determined before the non-sentient sex impinges on the consciousness. Anger, frustration, hopelessness, apathy listlessness, obsession, aberration, misanthropy, sociopathy, and blatant misogyny are all potential results. All of these are marks of unreason that can gain a foothold depending on many, many pre-existing conditions. It is just a matter of which form they take. Misogyny and frustration is almost always present in some form at some level. They also go hand in hand. The frustration with the sexual situation leads to unwarranted frustration with women, in general, which is just another way of saying misogyny.

For many, and this goes for both men and women, the perception has been drilled in that this life is always going to be a misery. That we should not expect anything but trouble in this life, and the best we can hope for is that things will get better after we are dead. ??!?! Errr, could you repeat that?

Initial conditions

Let's call it initial conditions. The conditions in a man's life when he begins to realize that he is not very good at sex. Is he pursuing a path of success in some particular field(leading to obsessions about power, fame, money)? Is he caught up in failure (leading to terrorism, homelessness, or hopelessness)? Have his role models caused further distortions?

The initial conditions, of course, go far deeper than that, including the essential character of the individual. Does the man have confidence in himself before the bane erupts? Is he already preconditioned by his role models to view women as lesser beings and victims? This does not even begin to touch on the preconditioning of the culture in which he lives.

The difficulty with analyzing initial conditions of this subject in depth is that, like the weather, the situation is complex in the extreme and has been developing for a very, very long time. The convolutions are endless. All that is being attempted here is to give a broad sense to the situation's complexity, some simple examples of how varied the outcome can be, what common characteristics may exist, and how much of it, at least, ties to non-sentient sex.

In these seemingly opposite paths through life, of extreme success and extreme failure, that portray the most extreme situations, are both affected by the ever-present bane of non-sentient sex, there is, at least, one similarity. A loss of integrity, dignity and self-respect leading to a lack of honour, courtesy, grace, responsibility and the joy and celebration of life. This is one of the primary hallmarks of non-sentient sex and it is imprinted deeply into society and reflected in all of mankind.

It is also possible that some men actually recognize the lack, the sexual inadequacy, at a more conscious level than this book portrays. There are some signs that some men strive in interesting, though unsuccessful, ways to achieve sexual adequacy. If such is the case, the effects of not reaching sexual adequacy are probably severe.

In all of this, it is worth noting that the distortions to personality that are embedded into children are also extremely complex, since they are deeply embedded secondary effects caused by exposure to distorted role models at the very beginning before critical thinking and discernment begin to develop.

The distortions are double-barreled in the case of children and their role models. The children are influenced by the sexual inadequacy of the father or father figure(s) and the sexual dissatisfaction of the mother or mother figure(s). The initial conditions induced in children have also evolved over the millennia.

Relationships untrammeled by non-sentient sex

In the early stages of life, before non-sentient sex has taken hold, most people go through a state of discovery concerning the opposite sex. This stage of discovery allows a person to find others that are relatively compatible. If the child is not already completely corrupted by the cultural ramifications of non-sentient sex, then this may unfold in a fairly rational manner.

This encourages the thought that, once humanity is rid of the devastating effect of non-sentient sex, relationships may be complete and rewarding on the first attempt. Maturity concerning the physical aspects of a relationship should combine with the maturity of the emotional aspects so that relationships flourish early and last long. Even in the face of some of the conditioning, it may very well fade to some extent in the absence of the scourge itself. That may be the case today with any man that never encountered the problem.

It is most likely that, at this stage in a person's development, even the fumblings, awkwardness, and outright fear concerning interactions with a the opposite sex are due to the innate realization that there is trouble ahead due to a sense, absorbed from the role models, that all is not right. The child's early osmosis of the feeling that something is wrong about relationships between men and women most often creeps into the picture very early.

This will all fall to ashes as men find that none of this holds true in the presence of loving sex.

Forces at work

There are many forces at work today to make the situation worse and the little sanity we had in the past disappear further. This is why it is so urgent for us to shed our blinders and see reality, and finally, embrace reason, besides the fact that another generation should just not have to go through this.

In the past, having children was a good thing. The more the merrier. Infant mortality and a human race that was still ensuring its ascendency over a world, required many children. This ensured that the man had sex pretty much as often as he pleased, since the woman was more than willing to have more children. In the absence of lots of children *and* the lack of pleasure, it becomes less interesting.

The accelerating awareness, openness, and intelligence of the human race, is also making it clear to more and more people that something is wrong in the sexual arena and they are seeking alternatives in droves.

The overall dissatisfaction is beginning to run deep and it is causing havoc as we accelerate towards an existence including knowledge, capability, and expansion. Unreason is distorting everything we attempt to achieve due to our desperate attempt to outrun non-sentient sex. True satisfaction between a man and a woman, for an intelligent, sentient race, is the only recourse.

Transmission

This is the most difficult aspect for mankind to understand. Unreason spreads like a virus that can change its form and adapt almost at will, once the infection is present. All it takes is the initial conditions of loss of self-respect and the enabling of unfettered deceit.

The primary condition that releases the unreason is the feeling of sexual inadequacy of the male. Once that happens the virus of unreason is unleashed and it immediately begins to change its form and expands to infect everything in his life. Life's foundations are rocked. Now, contemplate the many and varied forms that it can take over millennia.

Conditioning

The conditioning is also a most difficult piece of this situation to explain. The discovery of all of this, of course, was quite shocking, but the conditioning was just extraordinary to overcome. Being able to peer through all of the conditioning of so many aspects of life was a long process. That is what made the last, most disabling conditionings concerning non-sentient sex so very shocking. Armed with a general distrust of so much of what had been seen in this life of humanity, to find something so hidden in one's own subconscious and finally realize that it was a pervasive delusion was completely staggering. In this instance, the belief that it was a widespread problem was so unbelievable. It took a tremendous amount of study to finally believe it. It is still difficult to believe.

Even with a natural distrust of so much of the human condition and the proclamations that everyone takes for granted, it was still difficult to believe that something so disturbing could be buried in one's own subconscious. Removal of the conditioning is still in progress.

When this idea was first encountered, that many struggle for a lifetime with sexual inadequacy and what that might represent, it was almost impossible to accept. It was like tearing a curtain away only to find a brick wall behind. That just goes to show how deep that conditioning is.

Since then, in discussions with quite a few people, it was fascinating to watch the walls go up at the slightest mention of sex. Just the word 'sex' itself has been conditioned into society to repel the brain from thinking about it. As if even the mention of the word sends up warning flags all over the place. Everyone finds it nearly impossible to talk about it.

It is recognized that there are cultures in the world in which sex may not be quite the pariah that it is in some of the western world. India comes to mind as a possibility. India is one of the few cultures (only?) in the world that openly recognizes that sexual satisfaction of both genders is in order due to the teachings of Kama Sutra. But, the evidence is not entirely clear and it was investigated to some extent.

How to try to describe it? It has been pounded into us from birth, not just in words but by example, that sex is not ever to be discussed. More than that, that it is a shameful subject, if not also a curse and something inherently bad. Getting into the details is more difficult than pulling teeth. The only saving grace is that there is, finally, a real solution. This is expected to finally drop the no longer necessary barriers to discussion, though it may still take a generation or two. The embarrassment of the outcomes of non-sentient sex is the reason for all of the barriers.

It is so very important that we not only start having loving sex, but also, be aware of just how important it is. The barriers brought on by conditioning, have to fall to accelerate this process of becoming sentient, as well as explore the true nature of sentient, loving sex openly.

The questions that surround

There are a number of the questions that led to this book. This is an abbreviated list. While any single question can be answered in a number of ways, only one answer satisfies all.

The assumption is being made that you have the knowledge to answer each question, now, on your own. The answers are not given, except in the form of this book, only the questions.

Keep in mind that, if there is one thing that is completely clear, it is terribly difficult to admit the lies and face the truth, especially when it hits so close to a person's self-esteem and self-image. The barriers due to conditioning, in the face of non-sentient sex, are immense. It is extremely difficult to accept in any form. For everyone, it is a matter of deep conditioning, since childhood, that needs to be swept aside.

While all of the dots connect, the detail of the connections are also not all explicitly mentioned. There are a lot of dots. You may wish to do some connecting and questioning for yourself.

Let's start with this question. Why are there so few relationships that last and flourish? While there are a number of relationships that last, they mostly last through nothing but inertia. Separate beds and no passion is the norm. Of course, that is only for those relationships that last. In most cases, it is just matter of convenience rather than a celebration of the relationship.

Why are men generally so awkward around women, especially when they are young? It just deteriorates or mutates from there in many cases.

On a similar subject and, maybe the most suspicious question, is the awkwardness concerning the talk between man and boy on the subject of sex. Why would this discussion be awkward? It would be astounding except that the man has little to say. It is the situation in which the blatantness of our inability to rise above our animal nature becomes most pronounced, other than when in be with one's woman. It is when the lack of having progressed from the brutish state becomes most apparent.

Why do men want to shower women in gifts, and yet, also, created misogyny? Why do women spend all of their time shopping, what's missing in their lives?

Why is it that men, in particular, are particularly vulnerable to aberrance, obsession, and a long list of various psychological damage? What could possibly be so close to the self-image of a man as to cause the unreasonable approach to life that is so evident in the daily existence? Why are men so competitive?

Why is it that unreason seems to be dominated by men? Why is it that these tendencies accelerate post-pubescence? What is really the cause of a mid-life crisis? Why is it that men don't ever seem to mature while women do? Why is it that many men use all kinds and forms of alternatives to please their lady other than the most direct form of sexual satisfaction - coitus, sexual intercourse? Why do men so often delve into perverted sexual situations? The list of questions in this area is extensive.

Why is it that the little blue pill is such a hit, even at an exorbitant price?

Why is it that there is such an obsession with pornography, in particular among men? Why does the sex trade exist?

Why is it that so many young men can be seen to transform from bright-eyed bushy-tailed young men to cynical men with frozen smiles finally to completely jaded individuals with no sensitivities left as they age? What disappointment in life could be so overwhelming to often cause this transformation?

Why would men in very supposedly successful situations become so disillusioned with life and so obsessive with their success? Why is it the oft-accepted view that life should be misery in a rather benign universe? In a brute animal species, this may be true. In a species that has completely conquered its environment, how can this possibly make sense? Why the transference from actual joy to some substitute obsession that is clearly lacking?   What is missing from those lives?

What flaw in the life of humanity could lead to our chaotic existence? What aberrant trait could cause us to look at existence as misery?   What faulty trait leads so far back into the earliest appearance of mankind as a sentient race that it would be accepted as the natural state?

What could be so destructive to the self-image of a sentient race? What changed between all the other animals of the planet and mankind? What didn't?

Why are men generally so compulsive?   Why are women generally so serene? Why are women so accepting? This line is fading in the modern world, but not in a good way.   Women are becoming more compulsive.   It is not men becoming less compulsive, obsessed with minutiae.

Why are men such "takers"?   Why are women such "givers"?   What could lead to the unreasoning violence, on all levels, of the male gender?

Why is any disruption within the home, worldwide ("What's the matter here" by 10,000 Maniacs), accepted and considered off limits? Worse yet, this destructive acceptance has been granted free rein within a country's borders, as well. That same "home boundary" expanded to the borders of a country.

There is some headway in this area and it would be interesting to see how much of that headway is due to women.

What is it that the male gender hides from at all costs? Why would the male gender try to hide from some particular fact? What could make men that seem to be doing very well in this world be so dissatisfied with themselves and their lives?

Why is it that men are focused on sex and women focused on love and security?

Why is it that so few people want to think? Why do so many people want to just shut down their ability to think? While education is held up as important, which of course it is, it clearly does not enable well educated folks to really think. Thinking and education are often very distant relatives. Why are the aberrations just as apparent in the most intelligent of our race as all others? Also, all strata of society have their quirks. Why is that?

What could lead to a society of insensitivity towards its other members, especially by those that have accrued the most success in worldly things? What leads to the obsession for worldly things? What causes the grasping? What causes the sociopathy that is so prevalent in our societies, especially in the upper echelons that have substituted success for joy?

Why is it that, across all strata of society, relationships between men and women fail so regularly and utterly? Why are the majority of marriages either failed or miserable?

Why is it that, once, in the very distant past of our race, as humanity became self-aware, women were often cherished to the point that matriarchies and symbols of fertility, represented by pregnant women, were abundant? Why did it disappear? What caused the crushing force that relegated women to the state of second-class citizens treated like little more than cattle, at some time in the distant past? Did sentience have an effect?

What traits, besides intelligence and sentience distinguishes us from the other animals of the planet? In what ways have we not changed? What makes us seem, in many ways, just like a brute animal that can speak? What, due to mankind's sentience, did mankind become aware of that could have changed the situation so radically?

Why is it that religions always seem to have been a major force to make women of so little importance that, in many cases, it amounted to little more than persecution? Why is it that prophets are almost always *portrayed* as sexless men with no women in their lives? Why are men predominant in all aspects of public life?

Why is sex so very suppressed in society? This, maybe more than anything else, is baffling. Sex should surely be celebrated so why is it hidden in a dark corner as if we are ashamed of it? It is truly like something about its animal origins disturbed us. It is surely as if some dirty little secret is being avoided. As if there is something concerning this very natural function that disturbs us greatly, as a sentient race. Something prevalent enough to make us shy away from mention of anything concerning it. Keep in mind that it is the single most important function of humanity that allows us to continue to exist. Keep in mind, also, that it is the most transcendent physical joy that can be attained - *or should be*. What could possibly be impeding that joy and celebration of life? Why is it not the unimpeded joy it should be?

What could possibly have caused all of the bizarre paradigms that permeate society? How can it be that some of the paradigms, at the most basic level, permeate society worldwide. What could have been so prevalent in society throughout the ages that it would lead to paradigms suppressing any mention of sex and distortions concerning the activity?

Why is it that, as a rule, men do not share secrets? Women are known for sharing their concerns, issues, and secrets with other women. What impedes men from doing the same? It's a natural enough tendency to want share in order to resolve issues. What holds men back from this ability to share?

Why do men often seek domination? In particular, domination of women, often mistreating them horribly? Why do people (especially men) seek unfathomable amounts of money and power, since it is fairly obvious that it does not really satisfy? The obsession is unreasonable, a distraction. What are they distracting themselves from?

Why does all speculative fiction never suggest any fundamental change to the way we do things, who we are as a race? As with so many of the other oddities, it is as if speculation, when it comes to mankind, is stifled. Why is it some of the male speculative fiction writers predict the end of the male gender?

Why do many women, after a few encounters with men, turn to women for sexual satisfaction? Why do many men, after a few encounters with women, turn to men for sexual satisfaction? Both seem to be in increasing number. Why do so many religions suppress sex and provide bizarre rituals concerning the act? Why do so many religions frown on anything that might be considered fun?

Why is there a tradition of not having sex before marriage? What does this inexperience, especially of the woman, conceal? Why is it that many men are such thrill-seekers? How is it that, though some man or woman is attached to someone, they "fall in love" with someone new?

In a very general sense, why don't we have a society that encourages the welfare of all? This is the intelligent, beneficial (win-win?) thing to do for humanity, as a whole. It seems a natural progression from a sentient state.

Why is it that some religions (many?) treat sex like the plague, like a sin? Why is it that some religions consider enjoyment and pleasure to be such a curse? Is this just a confirmation of the most basic feelings on the subject? Why is so much tied up in the afterlife?

What happens to so many people when they break up with someone? Why do both feel like they must have been unworthy or blame the other person wholeheartedly for the failure?

A final question in this section. What can be more devastating to a man than to have his self-confidence blown to bits just as he is reaching maturity? Worse yet, blown away in a way that he has been conditioned to ignore?

Connecting the dots

It is now so easy to answer all of those questions and identify the causes of all those weird behaviours. All of those behaviours of men concerning sex and all of the reactionary behaviours for women are crystal clear when viewed in context of disconcerting sex. All of the baffling behaviours of mankind begin to make sense. In other words, the questions needed to be compiled while a search went on for something that answered all of them.

We have lived with the burden for so long, so it seems natural. As has been pointed out before, it is natural for a non-sentient species! It is just that we have transcended what passed for the natural state of animals a long time ago. We just have to come to grips with that. Sentience is such a huge leap for nature, it should not be surprising that there are adjustments to be made.

Turning point

If one looks at the world today, one can see that we are reaching a critical turning point. All of the nonsense of our forefathers is being thrown out. We are attempting to recognize reality, as painful as that process is. We are seeking the real answers, finally. It is to be expected that we will take mis-steps. But we are finally maturing.

A continued misinterpretation of the answers to the fundamental questions, at this time, could be disastrous. We are playing with toys well beyond our ken, wisdom, and maturity.

As has always been proven throughout history, mankind is smarter than many influential cynics ever give it credit, writing mankind off as nothing more than trained apes.

With our future at stake and the sandbox so filled with toys of unimaginable power, danger and potential destruction, it is essential that we grow up. While the hue and cry for maturity, peace, love, etc are easy to proclaim, it does not really satisfy by itself. It is not enough.

Fermi Paradox

The Fermi Paradox, in short, suggests that there should be intelligent species that have filled every corner of the cosmos after 13 billion years of the universe's existence. Of course, there are many suggestions on why this hasn't happened, from speculation that we are the only intelligent species in the universe to speculation that every species that attempts sentience and progress destroys itself in some way. There is also the suggestion that life may have just started later than any assumption suggests. This is, maybe, where Santayana's direct quote makes the most sense. Every time mankind has thought itself the center of the universe, we have been disappointed. The solar system does not revolve around our world, the universe does not revolve around mankind.

Considering our own situation, the struggle to become the dominant race on our planet and the necessary impetuses of nature (e.g. sexual drive), it is easy to believe that most supposedly sentient races continue down a path of self-destruction due to their inability to accept some single fact concerning their own existence. There was some striking difference from their predecessors that must be acknowledged and dealt with that never is; thus never overcoming the distortion and becoming full sentient and opening the way to sapience.

No advanced species comes into existence on its own. It is always the result of a great deal of evolution. The inability to overcome some factor from their less evolved past drives them unwittingly to their own end.

.It seems much more likely that we will find the last remnants of intelligent alien races that never actually embraced their sentience strewn across the universe rather than some rabid, war-mongering alien race that has not destroyed itself. A war-mongering race that does not eventually destroy itself seems a contradiction in terms.

In our case, that factor is our sexual conundrum and that may be the standard stumbling block for many races endowed with sentience. Sex fits the bill perfectly for the mechanism to evolve a race to the point of ascendency. It could be a very common form of procreation for a sentient race. There are certain aspects of sex, such as the potential for diversification of genes and new traits (i.e enabling evolution), as well as other possible aspects, that are essential in the development of a sentient race.

Removing the blinders that have been donned due to our emergence as a sentient race is necessary to transcend the past. In our case, at least, it is the transcendence of the sexual imbalance and paradox that will overcome the scourge of unreason. Sex is our very nature. Satisfactory, and satisfying sex is our transformation beyond the other animals into something that deserves to be sentient.

The answers

The insight that this book is attempting to convey is not even surprising. It is inevitable as we seek answers, and also, that we uncover inconsistencies in humanity's story. We are bursting forth from this planet of our birth, and coincidentally, we are gaining momentum in understanding ourselves and the universe in which we live. It is not an easy universe. We need to be prepared for any eventuality that the unknown can provide. We must be able put away our fear, our gibbering in the dark haunted by a mistake we made long ago, in order to be able to do so. We must put away our unreason. The single challenge of non-sentient sex that we have not faced has been a burden beyond measure and it is still distorting every aspect of our existence.

There is no other probable cause for our unreason. Acceptance of unreason as impossible to remedy is just not sufficient. The universe isn't causing our misery, mankind is. It has to stop.

Ripples and tidal waves

One has to look very deeply into the nature of existence to be able to glimpse the full ramifications of inadequate sexual expression. One must realize that the elimination of non-sentient sex from the human race would take a few generations to have its full effect. Children are influenced in their outlooks on life by the role models in their lives. Most importantly, they imprint from their parents or closest guiding role models at a subconscious level. As mentioned earlier, it is hoped that, without the final trigger of sexual inadequacy and, in its stead, loving sex for both involved, that the insupportable, irrational model will begin to collapse of its own accord within a single generation. But, due to the depths to which it driven in some instances and the scars left behind, as well as the breadth of society's behaviour that it affects, it will certainly take more than one generation to completely heal.

The trouble with troubles

As one is reading this book, it is very likely that a number of troubles of mankind will come to mind. Along with that trouble, it is very likely that the idea will be entertained that this is an important trouble, also, so why should non-sentient sex and the suppression of sex be such a big deal? That is one of the reasons that behavioural mechanisms, the questions that surround, and the term root cause were all introduced.

Throughout this book, a number of other troubles of mankind were scrutinized to some extent and it is clear that they are secondary, or tertiary behavioural mechanisms, unexplainable on their own and completely baffling outside of the context of non-sentient sex. They are not sources but outbreaks of unreason.   Only one trouble answers all of the questions concerning the unreason of mankind. Non-sentient sex. It is a root cause for the vast majority of our unreason.   If not the only one, it is surely a primary root cause for our unreason. In the fifty or so years of study of the unreason of mankind, not a single other trouble was identified that stands on its own.   That doesn't, of course, mean there isn't one but it does make it seem highly unlikely that a trouble of similar scope and importance will be found that stands on its own.

There certainly have been other troubles in the past of some scope. Even the struggle for survival of the human race and the individual being cannot be compared.   While a driving factor, it is not something that engenders unreason. Also, the individuals that no longer struggle for survival still suffer from unreason just as much as anyone else, no matter where they are on the social ladder. The same can be said of the human race, as a whole.

We have conquered everything we face except for our own unreason, because we have not faced it. We turn away from a close inspection of the self-image of the individual, as well as mankind, leaving it as uncharted territory. We have masked it in the past with unsuccessful forays into the surface problems, completely mystified by the fact that we continue irrationally down the road of existence. 'We have nothing to fear but humanity itself' seems to be the accurate phrase.

The suppression, inhibitions, and guilt that surround sex are the most evident example of surface issues that we have avoided delving into deeply due to the fear of what will be found. They are secondary behavioural mechanisms driven by the unreason caused by non-sentient sex. They are also critical to our ongoing unreason since they reinforce the behaviours and conditioning that lead to the continuance of non-sentient sex and block any attempts to overcome the inadequacy.

Sex itself is surely an essential part of nature and cannot be removed without causing the end of any race that attempts to do so. Eliminating the root cause behavioural mechanism, though, that encourages irrational perceptions must be achieved by an intelligent race. To truly raise our race to the level that we seek, of sentience and sapience, we must rid ourselves of the aberrations and deficiencies attached to sex. Legislation, laws, and enforcement are nothing more than a stopgap. They are not an end game.

The end game is that everyone now should easily be able to do away with their own non-sentient sex and that, alone, will make the most necessary change. Everything else will be just a matter of how much we concentrate our efforts to resolve and admit to past nonsense.

Credentials

It seems, especially with non-fiction, that many people desire to see the credentials for writing on the particular subject at hand. Considering the subject, it should not come as a surprise that the credentials are ... unusual ... in the extreme.

The university degree is not in psychology or psychiatry. Of course, that was a necessity. Anyone that had been conditioned into viewing the world as "people are messed up and we need to fix it", like a mechanic fixes a car would have stopped me in my tracks. It took a deeper level of insight which these professions would have crippled. Any paradigms of significance would completely block the path to discovering the truth about sex. As it is, it took more than sixty years to overcome all of the conditioning. Maybe my highest qualification is I am a paradigm breaker by nature. I can sense them a mile away and avoid them at all costs.

The most important credential is that I am a polymath. I look into everything without exception - and attempt connections. I go through so very much information that just gets stored away and correlated in a way that is very hard to describe. That does not just include facts, but human observation. Observation of all of the various quirks of humanity that, invariably, raised red flags. It also includes the observation of many cultures around the world that I was blessed enough to encounter in all of my travels. Connecting all of the dots is the best I can do to explain what was done with all of that information.

The polymath knowledge was necessary to be able to leap to intuitive answers. It is not really intuitive but a constant attempt to connect the dots, followed by incessant testing and questioning of the connections to see if they are valid. Read "Blink" by Malcolm Gladwell if you desire to know how deep knowledge can give seemingly intuitive answers. I rather like the term synergist best for what I do.

I took a test, once, at work, that basically looked it two supposedly opposing ways in which to think. Creative, imaginative thinking and analysis paralysis. I nailed both of them to the vast surprise of the test administrators. That was not supposed to be possible.

This was essential. It is not enough to leap to conclusions. They must be tested, repeatedly. No conclusion should ever be fully trusted. Never. That is a trap. New questions, new viewpoints must continually be thrown at any supposition until none are left. When you have exhausted the questions and viewpoints, just wait awhile. There are always more. You would be amazed at how many possible alternative conclusions and thousands of pages of ruminations and testing I went through over the last forty years to get here. At some point, though, the most important conclusion begins to stand out and prove it has some degree of substance.

Secondly, I don't mind asking crazy questions. This is essential. You just have to be willing to consider them crazy until they pass every test. I guess I have always lived by the phrase that the Japanese stated so perfectly. "You may feel like a fool for a moment if you ask a question. You will feel like a fool for a lifetime if you don't." The crazier the question, obviously, the longer you may feel like a fool, unless it is one that is easily and quickly thrown out, which is usually the case. It should never be perceived as a wasted effort. If nothing else, it sharpens the skills. If the ultimate question is important and complicated enough, it is just another step along the way to final understanding.

This may not seem that important but most people fear crazy questions as if the questions themselves make them crazy. It only makes you crazy if you accept them without thorough analysis. It is the only way in which to attempt to connect disparate dots. The more experience at the method, the easier and more quickly one can throw out the questions that just don't work at all.

Thinking long term means thinking in terms of questions unanswered or not fully answered. It means being comfortable with unanswered questions. It means being extremely uncomfortable with soundbites that answer nothing. This is another way in which humanity seems to be devolving. Soundbites (think twitter) are the order of the day.

Never, ever trust an answer completely. There are always more questions. As I've mentioned elsewhere, I started by investigating our systems (e.g. institutional structures), and then, cultures. I spent years looking at each, but finally, had to throw them both out. They just didn't answer the fundamental question: why is mankind so very screwed up and what can we do about it? They only partially answered. But, they led the way to the insight that it is just people at the heart of all of our problems, individuals that, in groups, become institutions, cultures, and societies. Nothing beyond focus on the individual could ever answer why we are so irrational. It comes down to the individual.

Just like most of the current way that we deal with problems, these pieces were still looking from the outside, still blaming our problems on other external issues rather than humanity itself and its delusions. One that became clear was that the problem couldn't be with mankind, cultures, or institutions. To really identify and resolve our problems, it had to come down to something wrong with the individuals on a vast scale.

I try to think in terms of a hundred years as a short span of time. This is important in so many ways. Our current focus on the next fifteen minutes up to, on the outside, a quarter of a year is disastrous. Yes, of course, I believe it is partially due to our irrationality which is caused by …

I believe that giving reincarnation an outside chance is very, very powerful and would be the best concept to be adopted by mankind (though never believed thoroughly). If you think you're going to be back in this mania, once again, it gives you a powerful motivation to clean things up. Getting one's focus away from the minutiae of the moment is paramount. I am agnostic, in actuality. I don't believe one can know what's on the other side. It is just that reincarnation has the most benefits for *this* life along with a long theory about why any other choice to adopt just doesn't provide much benefit in this world or after.

Another qualification is my voracious reading of speculative (i.e. SciFi) fiction at its height, when thought-provoking ideas were in vogue. Asimov, Heinlein, Clarke, and so many more wrote stories that provoked thinking and speculation.

On the purely creative front, I studied scenario planning. Scenario planning is a way in which to attempt to peer into the future. It has been used in some very interesting ways to improve certain things.

Scenario planning usually is started by depicting some future state that might take place. From there, one looks for signposts along the way that indicate that this future state is beginning to emerge. Really, the main point of the exercise is to assess what is the best way to be prepared for this future state if it were to happen. In this case, it was not in any way a formal effort. Just a continuing attempt to peer at what would get us to the state, the situation, the status that we were no longer looking like lunatics, and acting like brutes. An idle speculation as to reasons for our very apparent irrationality viewed from a point that we were finally, really rational. What is the difference?

Believe it or not, one of my highest qualifications is I write poetry. I get into this more in the Final Word but let me just add that, not only did it help me gain the necessary insight but, it also helped me keep my sanity while I searched. Ummm, if you get a chance, read "The Travelers" and think Great Heart.

Then, there are the questions, some of them quite crazy. I've already gone through some of the pertinent questions that filled my mind. When you surround an issue with enough questions and enough knowledge, it is almost a certainty that you will find an answer. Just don't ever convince yourself it is the final answer or the final question.

The primary driving factor, though, was that I could never accept that the human race was so unbelievably screwed up. It has always mystified me that we just accept the situation. Thank goodness I am quite comfortable in my own head. Trying to discuss any of this with anyone was just impossible. It just doesn't seem to gain traction with anyone I have ever met. There were a couple of people that would tolerate it just out of respect but no one with whom to really discuss these types of questions (and much simpler ones, in fact) and speculation.

A critical credential is that I had the time and luxury to dig deep and thoroughly into the problem for the last decade. I quit a very lucrative job for the purpose of making sense of all of the nonsense I had seen. No, I can't say I was planning on solving one of the biggest conundrums of mankind's existence but I did want to take a step back and look at the big picture. There was just a background feeling that something very, very important was missing.

Also, essential to this effort was that I just love puzzles. Sherlock Holmes, Agatha Christie, chess, anything that was an attractive puzzle, though I became bored with them all very quickly as I realized the puzzle of mankind outdid them all. And, as I mentioned earlier, being a criminal detective or solving any lesser problem has no lasting effect. There are always more criminals. Even if I couldn't solve the puzzle, it was just such a fascinating effort! it was the only puzzle really interesting and complex enough to make the effort worthwhile. I really expected that it would last a lifetime! And, to my utter dismay, it actually might.

I think that my career of engineering and marketing (a very weird combination) along with my unremitting bent towards strategy and viewing everything from a 40,000 foot level had a lot to do with it, as well. The puzzles, both technical and human, that I solved during those years were very rewarding and mentally stimulating.

Santayana's quote has always rattled around in my head. Knowing what went on in history just didn't seem to cut it. Once again, there was something missing.

In summary, the times were right for such a discovery and my background just fit the bill.

Right angle thinking

Right angle thinking is hard to describe. It is almost like an ability to detach the mind from the mundane view that is presented to it on a daily basis. I suggested, once, that it is like looking to the left while still looking right.

I have always been skeptical and suspicious of any paradigm. As an example, when everyone is convinced that the human race is just nutso (clinical term) with no recourse then they must be right, right? That violence and insane views are just the way it is and that should be accepted. I have always been skeptical of these "truths", not in a conscious way just complete distrust for all of the platitudes that are cast about so easily.

To me, mankind is awesome with awesome potential. There is some crazy shit going on out there and it doesn't have anything to do with reality.

Many have considered me crazy over the years but it was water off a duck's back because all I had to do was look around and it was easy to say, "It's not me that's crazy". All of the vituperativeness that surrounds us? *That's* nutso.

What was really necessary to get to this level of understanding was saturation. I needed to saturate myself in the depths of what was wrong with humanity. I spent the last decade or so contemplating the human condition and it's motivations.

The damage done

Over my lifetime, I have done a lot of damage to myself. Two or three concussions in the teen years, a car wreck that severely damaged my back and plenty of other damage. That is not even to mention the psychological damage. Like a dad that was a verbal terrorist, dominating and domineering the family along with my own rather unusual situation within that family. I am only skimming the details here. There was a lot of damage done.

I only mention this because what I ended up doing was trying to figure out what the hell happened to my life. How did I end up where I was? It was astonishing to me. By every right, my life should have been bliss. What was missing? There is no way that my life should have turned out as it did. It was a mess and there was no reason for it that I could determine. I started digging. I identified all of the damage done, such as those mentioned above, and it still didn't satisfy. It just didn't make sense. Something seemed to be missing. Lo and behold, it was loving sex that was missing. Even I, as much and as completely as I adore women, spent a great deal of my lifetime shattered when it came to women. It took nearly a lifetime to finally even realize it! When I realized that, it all came home to roost. I sucked at sex.

Overcome it all

Now, I have the desire to overcome it all. That's not so simple, and as I said earlier, I don't even know if it is possible to overcome all of the disturbed thoughts of a lifetime. At my age? I should know better, right? Next life, right? And, there, we get to the final driver of the discovery of this problem. There was no way in hell I wanted to come back to the same mess in the next life. Besides, I made a promise to someone.

Make no mistake

The multiple entendres in this subtitle should make you pause in thought. What it is truly talking about is that I realize there is some slight chance that I am overblowing some aspects of these insights concerning non-sentient sex and sentient love (still looking for a chagrin emoticon). I hope you see that is due to my belief that nothing is ever really finally, thoroughly answered until it has come to fruition rather than any really substantial doubt. There is little doubt left in my mind as to the momentousness of this change. I expect most of you will agree if you've gotten to this point in the book. The biggest question, which is answered and confirmed for me, is just how many others have disturbances to their thought processes similar to mine and it is caused by non-sentient sex. How many are affected by this scourge is well confirmed for me. I believe it is closer to 90% of men but that will be confirmed as time progresses and 30% is certainly enough to cause the described upheaval of the human race. How many are disturbed, their self-regard compromised in some form, is also convincing. This is a problem of massive proportions. The specifics of the conclusions will slowly emerge.

Quandaries

The writing of this book presented a number of quandaries and challenges that I think I have finally overcome in this ninth revision (before ever publishing).

The writing of this book was part of the learning process involved concerning the whole subject. It was used as the template to set down the proposals, and then, attempt to tear them apart and test them until there were no serious issues left to be considered. I had many questions and reservations left through, at least, five of those revisions. It became apparent, in the early revisions, that humanity's conditioning was a huge force. Of course, one of the biggest challenges was to find a real solution for men's stamina. All of what I found through study of existing suggestions were just delaying the inevitable (ejaculation) and I almost accepted this (paradigms, again) but it just wasn't a solution.

Everything in this book was dependent on finding a real solution. Otherwise, it was just pointing out a problem without a solution. I would never have published in that case. The puzzle would not have been completely solved. The world has enough angst without another insanity without resolution.

The book itself and the way in which to introduce the subject matter became paramount since it became clear that people were just so repulsed by any discussion of the subject of sex, due to conditioning, and that it was both genders. It became fascinating how deeply embedded were the notions, in both sexes, that this was not a subject that could be discussed. When the discussion was forced, the mind basically shut down and retrenched into the conditioning and paradigms installed.

I attempted to prepare the reader with the story of searching for the nail before introducing the real topic of discussion. It still happened. People would turn off on page 26 as the word sex was first used.

The subject matter needed to be introduced in a new format. This is the format that I chose and it seems to work for most. I hope it works for you.

Final Word

Some may say that it just seems too simple, too easy. Please tell that to all of the human inhabitants of this planet over the last three thousand years. It is like many things in retrospect.   Some of my favorite examples of retrospective simplicity are velcro, that new type of can opener, and The General Theory of Relativity.   In retrospect, they all make sense once the facts are laid out and examined. The more complex and radical the concept, the more difficult it is for people to accept. General relativity was initially considered nonsense.

One of the keys to unraveling any mystery is being unbound by the paradigms that have been handed down, generation to generation.   That is, in essence, The General Theory of Relativity and the new type of can opener.

You have to throw the book out. In this case, for me, that was easy. I could not tolerate the nonsense and I ignored all temptations to find some lame excuse as aberrant and distasteful.

I hope this book has also given you just some slight sense of the depth and breadth with which I pursued the conundrum of mankind's disturbance. Believe me when I say, the best that can be hoped is that you developed only a sense of the effort that was put into this and the massive number of dots that were connected over a period of about fifty years.

I found writing this book so very fascinating. I went into this book fighting it every step of the way.   I had no desire to write a book.   I was more than content writing my poetry. I have written close to a thousand poems, each one with strict rhyme and attempted rhythm.   The thing is that the poetry, for me, is about concept discovery and it is a fascinating process.

There is no doubt it led to the final insights that are detailed in this book. I have always liked discovery of ideas that benefit.   The problem, though, is coaxing those ideas out. Some people do it by "sleeping on it" (I have done this, also, but it doesn't seem as reliable for getting to the deep truths of life for me). But, poetry!

What I finally understood was that I get so caught up in figuring out the rhyme and the rhythm of the poem that the ideas flowed freely, unimpeded by the normal clutter of everyday thought. This was clear when the final results of the poem had nothing to do with the initial ideas I had going into the poem. Those deep thoughts that were bubbling away in the back of my mind but not finding a way to be conveyed, would express themselves through the vehicle of my poetry.

That is not the reason I started writing poetry. The reason for that was love of a woman.   There are a number of these poems in the book named, "Serendipity".   There is another set of love poems that you will probably never see.   These were written for a different woman at a much later point in life.

They are hers and hers alone.   If she wishes to publish them, that is fine. Otherwise, you will not ever see them. I'm not expecting them to be published ever.

But, this book was a totally different effort. By the time I started the effort of writing the book, it was no longer the development of new ideas.   That previous work was what might be termed an intuitive effort.   When enough breadth and depth of knowledge in an area (does that give you a clue as to the necessary effort in understanding the breadth and scope of human behaviour and history?), the answers just *seems to* appear. It is that scope of knowledge and, in this case, the many dots being connected, that makes the answers appear. I *knew* what was going on thoroughly, especially once I had rewritten the book the first two or three times.

Then, it was a matter of rewriting it another six times to make it discernible to everyone else and laying any of my own last doubts to rest. It is interesting, though, that, as the explanation became more coherent, so did my confidence in the answer.

I have a deep distrust of most of the nonsense of mankind going back to my youngest days.   And, describing what was really going on was now paramount. The book was the very awkward, uncomfortable effort of conveying those ideas to others. It is difficult to convey ideas of any kind but the radical ideas that I often develop are, well, life has taught me to be cautious. Too many skeptical looks, cautious interactions and reactions from friends, as well as the distancing of such friends, all taught me that ideas are not most people's forte today or in the past. That is a shame, it should be the forte of everyone alive. That's fine. I expect it will be changing rather rapidly now. Yes, I think that the irrational thought brought on by non-sentient sex has also impeded our ability to think. If you think it through, you will agree (that's a Cheshire cat's grin you are sensing floating all by itself in the air in front of you). I'll skip the long theory involving economics, automation, and the long term goals of humanity that make this the perfect time for the majority of mankind to begin thinking.

I knew it would be a prodigious chore to overcome the ingrained biases and resistance to new vistas. So, the book would need to be written very, very well. It would need to *flow*. I sure hope it *flow*s as well as I desire. Did I ever mention how much I love double entendres?

Since I was already proficient at writing poetry, I was always making comparisons. In some ways, the efforts were exactly the same. In others, they were polar opposites. The effort of crafting was exactly the same. The finger-tip use of dictionary and thesaurus and word processing software (and rhyming dictionary, in the case of poetry) were such a vast improvement over the tools our poor ancestors endured as to make for a powerfully intuitive enhancement to the writing process in either case. I mention this for the younger generations that may not comprehend how fortunate their situation is. It is also worth attempting to convey just how much this all could help the acceleration of the intellect of mankind if the tools are used as commonly as they should be.

The forms were different and the necessity of conveying ideas versus discovering ideas was radically different. There was also the fact that the poetry was never really written for anyone but me. It was like an additional process or two that was added on when writing the book. Not only was I required to suggest an idea but, also, confirm the veracity of the statement and elucidate the concept well. What a pain! That is, the discovery of insights in my poetry were for my own edification no one else's and, if they weren't explicit that was fine. Even worse, the needs of writing poetry almost requires cryptic statements which, I battled through four or five versions of the book. I had to be clear, not cryptic, when writing the book. And, as I conclude the book, it is still true. I'd rather be writing poetry. Ahhh, to write reams of poetry for Infini Entendre, once again! Did I mention I like double entendres?

The romantic poetry, of course, was very different indeed. It was written for two women that I adore and always will. Those poems were of a different nature and are easily understood by the one for whom they are written. Well, mostly, anyways. The ones that will probably never be published are, by far, the finest poetry I've ever written. My heart was in that situation completely and still is.

Sorry for the digression. You see? When I first started writing the book, it was just like this. It was my random thoughts rather than a directed effort to open the eyes of mankind. It was cryptic, yet insightful just like the poetry. Up until I started writing the book all of my writing (other than poetry) was a deep delving into ideas that sounded attractive but needed study and only I had to ever read it. The ideas needed to be written down and really scrutinized. They never needed to make sense to anyone but me. Heck, a lot of it ended up making no sense at all after scrutinization. Two of those ideas were important to lead the way to the cascade of ideas that finally encompassed the human dilemma of sex but they were not final answers. Writing them out and pondering them were critical to getting there. Those were the studies of institutions and culture. What became blindingly apparent was that these were just results, by-products of the real problem because the real problem resided within the individual. They were surface issues.

While this may seem like a digression for my own edification, it is not. The woman that I have learned to adore over the last year (Ahhh, Serendipity!) and the development of that adoration was essential, in the strangest ways, to the development of this book. So, maybe, this is the one acknowledgement that I can make (rather than a whole section. Errr, not to forget the very useful help of my son!). This woman is so playful and requires such an enormous use of intellect to celebrate, that it inadvertently sharpened everything about my efforts. She also increased the level of revel involved in, well, everything. Just when I had about given up, her very existence drove me on and enhanced the clarity and joyfulness of the effort (kinda like my poetry always has!). Which is very weird indeed since, in many ways, it has been one of the most distressful situations I have ever faced. But, even so, the joy incurred would not relent and never will.

So then, under the conditions of a most strange life, I couldn't help but stumble across the real problem. I can sum it up by saying that I adored women. Always have, always will. But, two women taught me the essence of womanhood and femininity. All women are, by nature, serene and wonderful. Yes, many are distorted by the influence of men but, at the very heart of what it is to be a woman, it is serenity. But, these two women are the essence of everything beautiful in life.

Anyways, that was fact number one of my life. Fact number two was that I sucked at sex. Worse than that, I was filled with all of the nonsense of conditioning that covered up how bad I sucked at sex. This set up a conflict that never ended until I discovered the essence of this book. More than that, it didn't really end until I found the essence of the remedy to the problem. The simplicity of the remedy still shocks me but what an immense relief!

The discovery of the problem, as well as its resolution, changed everything for me. I regained the unlimited confidence in myself that had slowly been whittled away by the scourge of incompetent sex and the derangement that goes along with it. Unfortunately for me, it happened at such an age that the results were less than magnificent on the physical front. No longer was I limited in my capability but, now, I was limited by age. Great. That was okay. It was just a matter of age, so just something with which I had to live, but I could live with that. It is the haunting specter of inability, incompetence when a man is wholly virile that shakes the foundations of manhood.

The unanswerable dilemma was finally resolved. All of my life I had adored women but couldn't satisfy them. Because I adored women so deeply, I could never convince myself that I was gay. I had a problem, that was all. It took forever to admit to the problem but, in the back of my mind, I knew. I may have hated being with them because I knew I would eventually fail to live up to expectations (my own, at least) but I still adored them ('can't live with them, can't live without them' takes on a whole new meaning in this context). The physical need for someone to hold and love never went away but I lived with the ache as best I could. Because I never had a problem with relieving the sexual pressure through, ahem, whatever means were 'at hand', the pressure never overcame my rationality.

So, here I was with the answer to the problems of mankind without a way to convey the message. As I wrote and rewrote the book, it was just like every significant effort of my lifetime, which included my poetry and my ongoing, late-in-life desire and effort to learn the piano, it just took a lot of significant effort to understand everything there is to know about the goal. In this case, it was conveying a message that could free mankind from its shackles. As I progressed in the task, it became apparent that it was more than that. It had to be conveyed in a palatable manner (believe me, the first few rounds were just rantings at the unfairness of it all and the despicability of the aberrations and obsessions that it caused as well as a lot of digressions and discontinuity). More than that, it had to be conveyed in a way that also captured the reader's attention. I hope to goodness that I have accomplished that, finally. This is ninth rewrite of the book.

What surprised me was that, after writing reams of thoughts and considerations on institutions and cultures that amounted to insights but not a final answer, this concept of inept sex really *was* the answer. Everything fit like all of the pieces of the jigsaw puzzle. The whole chapter on "The questions that surround" was to give just a clue as to how deeply I explored the issue and how all of the pieces of the puzzle, when taken as a whole, fit. That sub-chapter is just the tip of the iceberg with regards to questions answered. One thing I learned along the way of the fifty years of discovery is that it is always about the questions. Simple answers to a single question can be misleading in the extreme but, when you take a host of questions that surround an issue, then you can find a real answer that fits all of the pieces of the puzzle.

One of the biggest misperceptions to overcome was how common the problem is. All of the conditioning induces us to believe it is only a small problem and only a few people encounter the problem. But, it is absolutely certain that, at least, 30% of men are inept. Beyond that, it is reasonable to believe that 75% of men are inept and it is not out of the question that the number is closer to 90% or higher. What is absolutely flabbergasting is that the numbers are there in multiple studies and, yet, it has been brushed off due to our aversion to the subject matter.

As mentioned earlier, I have read books by John Armstrong, Eric Fromm, and Gary Chapman, as well as many others, both before and after discovering the insights contained in this book. It was fascinating to read them after conveying the ideas in this book. It also encouraged me that these insights are right. The level of confusion and frustration that pertains to the subject of love is staggering. Out of them all, I found Gary Chapman's "The Five Languages of Love" to be the most instructive. All of his concepts still pertain and have value. The other books and notes are instructive and insightful (very much so, in some cases) but it seems like a good rewrite is in order in most cases.

As I read all of these books and many more with the context of loving sex in the back of my mind, the more I wondered, though. They *all* made sense in the context of non-sentient sex. They all made so much sense that it makes one wonder if they ever would have been needed to be written in a world that had accepted loving sex. They are all forms of seeking the missing nail. Once the nail is found, then the desperate need to understand seems likely it should evaporate. We *will finally* understand.

The progression of this book was from a heap of partially conceived ideas and suspect paradigms and the relentless examination of these for veracity, to a clear comprehension of the foibles of our past. The biggest challenge was to gain an insight into what it could possibly be like without these impediments in our way. It is worse than even predicting the future. It was much more ambitious than the usual attempts at scenario planning. It is attempting to predict the future with a completely new, somewhat unknown set of variables in place. It was thrashing through even the simplest observations, such as mankind is essentially good and the universe is essentially benign. The conceptualization of what this could imply for the future were certainly lacking in scope. There is much to learn as we move forward.

Anyways, I hope you enjoyed the book. I also hope that it changes the human race in ways that we cannot even begin to imagine at this point but all are certain to be positive improvements. We are reaching out into the universe, now, in a big way. We have to do that in a manner that is fitting for a truly sentient race. I think the worst of the shackles are now revealed. The potential for shattering those shackles has been provided. There are plenty of hurdles left, such as eliminating all of the ponderous missteps that have led us down the wrong path. That seems a surmountable task. It will take will and effort. Those also should be available now that the human race is unshackled.

It must be reiterated, because it is just that important, that the search for male sexual adequateness should not be finished. While I am 99.999% sure (only the final implementation can make anything 100% sure) of the root cause of our unreason, I am only about 99% sure of the remedy. It should work if men can keep their heads and avoid their brutish nature but is that enough? I've also started to wonder if the phrase 'men don't twerk until the lady sings' does not need an additional component going something like, 'and the man needs to position himself high to arouse her fancy'. The phrase itself isn't be that big a deal, really. It's just that the talk between father and son has some significant points worth discussing now, instead of just being embarrassed with nothing to say.

It should be obvious that only a small sample could be studied to assure that the techniques of not twerking, going slow, and exercising the sex muscles was possible. I would not have published this book if the evidence was not considerable that the techniques overcome the lack. But, the surety will never be one hundred percent until it is a common practice and proved thoroughly. So, I beg mankind to assure that we have done everything that we can to assure that the solution is complete. I am 99% sure that it is for a number of reasons. The elegance reflects nature's way, the simplicity is such that anyone can learn it by word of mouth. It's perfect! Just not thoroughly proven. Until it is, it is of paramount importance to continue the search. Mankind conquers everything it faces as long as its wits are in tact. The cloak has been removed from non-sentient sex. The profit motive, for once, cannot be considered. A little blue pill will not cut it. It does nothing for the man's self-respect. We must convince ourselves thoroughly and utterly that the solution is complete. Not to worry, I'm sure the little blue pill will sell to old folks that need a rise. That's different.

Whickwithy can be found on Google+ I dearly hope that the community named Scenarios that can be found on my G+ account can be of use as a pool for any further knowledge or clarity, improvements or insights on sexual adequacy, as well as scenarios on how we undo all of the snarls caused by our past irrationality.

We cannot make rational decisions until we become a rational species. We cannot be a rational species until we completely resolve the conundrums of sex and the aftermath of non-sentient sex. Sapience is the final goal.

With the paralyzing effect on humanity of non-sentient sex gone, the transformation will be overwhelmingly auspicious. This may sound like hyperbole. That is a central challenge in attempting this book. The suggestion that something will change the world is consistently met with derision. It is the boy who cried wolf way too often. Too many times it has been shouted in the past. While there is no need to harp on the point, I can't help but mention it. I haven't the slightest shred of doubt left on the immensity of the impact of this change. Let the derision wait. I won't be proved wrong.

My own beliefs in the matter are that one hundred years from now, you won't hardly recognize humanity's behaviour it will have changed so drastically for the better. My belief is that man's natural state is goodness, curiosity and an unbounded interest in all that surrounds us. Not for the few but for the many. Most of this has already been proven utterly to me. I don't accept propositions easily. I accept this.

The feelings that come with self-acceptance and all of the outgrowths of love are amazing and unmatched by anything else in existence. It just shouldn't be so difficult to achieve.

You might want to call this Flower Power II. Some of us didn't give up. Finding the love of a particular one with whom to spend a lifetime will still be essential and far more fulfilling than it ever has been before, but it is difficult to determine whether this will be more easily done in the future or not. The problem is that I have some rather radical thoughts on this due to my life's experience. That life was certainly as clouded as anyone's due to the circumstances of non-sentient sex.   Whether this has also clouded my views on finding a particular person is too complex to determine without more effort than I care to impart.

I only found two women in a lifetime with whom I would really have cared to spend my life. Only one that gave my life light during the era after my sense was finally restored. As usual, the gaining of that sense and the arrival of that dear heart in my life were nearly coincident.   Serendipity doing her thing and now doing it in the form of a lovely Lady, a most feminine and womanly Lady. And, as far as I can tell, I still have a lot to learn. That is, after I gained enough sense to realize that the close tie between two people is like a kaleidoscope.

Where the whole situation becomes incredibly cloudy is this.   That woman embodies all of the amazing qualities of a truly sentient person.   She hides from that fact, she certainly has her problems, but she is truly sentient and struggles to achieve sapience more than anyone I have ever encountered.   She is so incredibly feminine and womanly, as well, that it makes my bones ache.

So, the problem is that what I expect to happen is that more people will begin to achieve this level in the near future. So, in that case, is it that people in general will become more acceptable as lovers?   That seems like the most rational expectation.   The common denominators for love to exist will become more prevalent. As the human race finally overcomes the hurdle, more people will be worthy of loving. But, there is something about this woman that I adore that, for me, is so incredibly special and I think goes far beyond just sentience and sapience. The best way that I can describe it is just that her nature makes a supernova of me. I could go further but it would be getting a little too intimate for these pages and it would fill another book. Actually, it has filled two.

As the first (and *only the first!!!*) to take this radical departure from the insanities of our past, it gives me the privilege to suggest some additional insights.   What our descendants will almost certainly discover and our future history should confirm is that looking at almost anything that has happened before this point, from all of the books, philosophies, form of entertainment, all of the cultures, institutions, history, and music, to the individual daily interactions will reveal themselves as something almost foreign.   The arts will be least affected. This is a huge break from all of the pain, disappointment, and heartache that mankind has always endured.   If you want to know how I could have ever developed the insights in this book, this reveals it. All of my lifetime, I lived in this foreign world as a foreigner.

As mentioned, the disruption of non-sentient sex and sentient love do not coexist easily. Isn't it wonderful and remarkable that there are two genders. One has suffered through the disorientation due to non-sentient sex almost losing the ability to embrace sentient love while the other has safeguarded humanity and the concept of love until it could be nurtured into full efflorescence.

It looks very likely that I won't be around long after the publishing of this book, so I have tried very hard to make the fifty years of study as clear as possible. Don't rely on anyone else (and, maybe, it is a good thing I will be gone; in fact, that is why I have used a pseudonym) to interpret this for you. Interpret it yourself and just feel assured that the pebble will turn into an avalanche of sentient love. Then, the foolishness of the past should be ended.

~W

Just because they fit this toil and trial of a lifetime so very well, a few of my poems. Believe me, I'd always much rather be writing poetry. The first poem, especially, was written under the reign of the woman that I adore and consider to be the personification of everything that is so fine about women. They are all some of the insights that led me here.

"The garden"

In the garden was the love, but not what most would think
A long and deepest draught of what it is one needs to drink
To fill the cornucopia, it starts along the spine
Emotions run the rampant way but never will refine
To read the book and feel the thrill, the essence in the touch
All the fire must be aflame, emotions follow such
The dwindling of delight is seen but never recognized
As dwindling of the kindle as the fire is compromised
No flame can burn so brightly and no love can ever shine
Unless the fire is quickened as it's felt along the spine

"Satisfaction"

The satisfaction that we all desire
The purpose that embodies life's own fire
The charge that sparks the reasons and the sight
That lights the candles beggaring the night
Is all contained within the sum of one
The woman lights the way like setting sun
True satisfaction comes without a cost
It is the transcendental that is crossed
The satisfaction now becomes the norm
Life and all its hardships now reform
When love, unbounded, blossoms all attune
That setting sun becomes as bright as noon

"Love"

The love, the greatest mystery of them all
Attempts without the ken assures the fall
It may well be that key unlocks the heart
But standing on one's own is where to start
No validation comes from the outside
Within one's heart is essence of the ride
Salvation does not lie within another
That search is sure to end in smirch and smother
The mirror must be faced with confidence
Feel the rhythm in the consonance
Then, the way is clear
To find that special dear
The study of this aspect is a challenge tantamount
To flying through the wilderness while riding catamount
The physical, the passion is what trumps the joker's jest
The senses should explode upon a pattern it expressed
The passions ride the tide unto conclusions that must sing
No good can be expected from piano with no string
The mental innervation is a minor, infant's test
The mirror, heart, and skin must fully feel the zing and zest
You need no one's approval but your own
Don't take a lifetime for that to be known

"Solutions"

A pulse is felt, it is enough, to navigate the day
A thrill runs through to fingertips assuring life's foray
But underneath, a rumble builds, its ramping all through time
There's more to this than just the thrill, there's more to life and rhyme
The singing of the universe is aching to get through
A tone that runs along the thread, vibrating me and you
The winding road of life leads to the insight of the view
'Tis not the road but in the dance we find the answer to
The questions that can build a life to something more than pale
To make each moment thunder, with a life that's strong and hale
The path is sometimes hidden, brush and brambles clog the way
The tune becomes more difficult, the dancing seems to stray
Solutions for the moment will become a tightened noose
To break the chains, reclaim the life, and ease the dancing loose
Solutions for eternity necessitate the deed
Requiring one to hold the course, to heal instead of bleed
But in the end, beginnings stir, the flower on the stem
Crowning life in something more, the hidden diadem
Now, the way is clearest and the path is smooth and straight
Just steady on, a patient heart, a will to now create
A view into eternity, essential to the task
The answer to the question mark before you ever ask
Seek the serendipity
A tempo set to destiny
Unending in its quality
All limits set by you and me
The rhythm's in wind and in the air
The steps must sense with loving and with care
Subtly posed, accept the steps in kind
No knowledge helps accept that life's divine

"The weaver and the wizard"

The artisan begins his tireless toil
The consequence of all the threads uncoil
The whisper of the weaver's patience tasked
Each thread, an answer to a question asked
But for the tapestry to answer all
The blend of threaded questions must enthrall
Suspended gaze must answer to the call
The witness of the wizard wherewithal
A tableau that can cast the curing spell
Eliminates inertias that propel
The tapestry unbinds the vile unreason
Transforming life from winter's brutal season
The weaver builds the tapestry from thread
The wizard conjures life for those undead
In colors bright, the tapestry portrays
That life can be much more than pending days
Warm and rich, this life beneath the sun
The weaver and the wizard are as one

CPSIA information can be obtained
at www.ICGtesting.com
Printed in the USA
BVOW11s0717080817

491446BV00002B/5/P